Improving Basic Services for the Bottom Forty Percent

A WORLD BANK STUDY

Improving Basic Services for the Bottom Forty Percent

Lessons from Ethiopia

Qaiser M. Khan, Jean-Paul Faguet, Christopher Gaukler,
and Wendmsyamregne Mekasha

WORLD BANK GROUP

Contents

Boxes

Figures

Tables

Foreword

When Ethiopia embarked on a program of improving service delivery by decentralizing power to the third, or *woreda*, level, we were initially skeptical. In the *World Development Report 2004: Making Services Work for Poor People*, we asserted that the delivery of basic services requires two things: First, citizens must be able to hold politicians accountable for allocating resources and monitoring results; second, politicians in turn must be able to hold service providers—teachers, doctors, nurses—accountable for quality delivery of services. We called these the two legs of the "long route of accountability." While Ethiopia's strong party affiliations and military traditions would make the second leg of the long route work well, the limited political competition at the national level potentially could weaken the first leg. Furthermore, whereas in principle decentralizing to the subnational level would make these accountability relationships work better—citizens would be closer to political leaders, and politicians could better monitor service providers—the limited capacity in some of the *woredas* could act as a brake on progress.

Our skepticism was unwarranted. Ethiopia has experienced a remarkable improvement in service delivery outcomes. Child mortality has fallen from 123 per thousand in 2005 to 88 in 2010, and the primary net enrollment rate rose from 68 percent in 2004/05 to 82 percent in 2009/10. This richly documented and analytically rigorous book explains why. While political competition at the national level remains limited, competition at the local level is healthy, with officials' career advancement depending on their being able to meet development and service delivery targets. The government has introduced social accountability mechanisms such as grievance redress through the Ethiopian Institution of the Ombudsman, financial transparency (the local budgets are posted in common areas), and citizen feedback on budget preparation and implementation. The government has also strengthened the second leg of the long route of accountability by recruiting teachers, health workers, and agricultural extension workers locally, and rates of provider absenteeism are now lower than in other countries in Africa. Greater citizen participation and the intrinsic motivation of people working in their local areas may have helped overcome the initially weak administrative capacity.

The relative success of Ethiopia's decentralized service delivery program is not a reason to be complacent, however. The achievements have arisen from a low base; Ethiopia remains one of the poorest countries in the world. The progress on indicators that people care about—students' learning and overall health status—has not been impressive. As these indicators are more specific to the individual, their achievement will require an even sharper focus on citizen voice and participation. Ethiopia has demonstrated how much can be achieved by opening up the system to greater accountability "from below." Just think how much more can be achieved by going further—and allowing poor people to participate fully in the delivery of services that are so important to them and their children.

Shantayanan Devarajan and Ritva Reinikka
Co-Director, World Development Report 2004

Acknowledgments

This book was written by Qaiser M. Khan (Lead Economist, World Bank), Jean-Paul Faguet (Professor for the Political Economy of Development, London School of Economics), Christopher Gaukler (Consultant, World Bank) and Wendmsyamregne Mekasha (Senior Social Protection, Specialist, World Bank).

This book is based on a World Bank report (84215-ET) developed with funding from the World Bank and a Trust Fund for Enhanced Supervision of Ethiopia's Promoting Basic Services program, supported mostly by the UK Department for International Development (DFID). That report benefited from suggestions provided by the peer reviewers—Robert Chase (Lead Economist, World Bank), Nazmul Chaudhury (Lead Economist, World Bank), Andrew Dabalen (Lead Poverty Specialist, World Bank), and Philip O'Keefe (Lead Economist, World Bank)—and other colleagues present at the review meeting, including DFID's Ethiopia Team, Andrew Goodland (Senior Agriculture Economist, World Bank), Ruth Hill (Senior Economist, World Bank), and Thanh Thi Mai (Senior Education Economist, the World Bank). Before the review meeting, Yoseph Abdissa (Senior Social Protection Specialist, World Bank), Colin Andrews (Senior Social Protection Specialist, World Bank), Carlo del Ninno (Senior Economist, World Bank), G.N.V. Ramana (Lead Public Health Specialist, World Bank), and Huihui Wang (Senior Health Economist, World Bank) also provided comments on the report. The authors would also like to acknowledge the technical guidance and advice received from Deon Filmer (Lead Economist, World Bank) and Lynne Sherburne-Benz (Sector Manager, World Bank). Members of the Ethiopian government who provided invaluable assistance include Ato Temesgen Walelign (Development Planning and Research Directorate); Ato Degu Lakew (Government Accounts); Ato Alemayhu Gebretsadik, Ato Biratu Yigezu, and Ato Habekristos Beyene (Central Statistical Agency); Ato Feta Zeberga (Ministry of Agriculture); Ato Asmelash Mersa (Ministry of Education); and Ato Wondimu Ayele (Ministry of Health and Economic Development). Support from Ato Getachew Negera, Head of Channel One Program Coordinating Unit (Ministry of Finance), is also gratefully acknowledged. Any errors and omissions are the responsibility of the authors.

We thank Shantayanan Devarajan and Ritva Reinikka, Co-Director, *World Development Report 2004*, for writing the foreword to this book.

Kavita Watsa and Chandrani Ray provided advice and assistance in the production of this book, which was edited by Kelly Cassaday and benefited from the support of Sofia Said, Team Assistant, World Bank. Gelila Wodeneh, Communications Officer, the World Bank also provided support and advice.

About the Authors

Qaiser M. Khan is Lead Economist working on Africa. He has worked on social protection and basic services for the poor at the World Bank since 1989, all over Africa, the Middle East, and Asia, and he has written considerably on the subject. Before joining the World Bank, he taught economics in the United States and worked for a management consulting firm out of New York and for a nongovernmental organization in Bangladesh. He has a PhD and two master's degrees from the University of Pennsylvania in Philadelphia, Pennsylvania, United States, and a bachelor's degree from Colby College in Waterville, Maine, United States.

Jean-Paul Faguet is Professor of the Political Economy of Development at the London School of Economics. He is also Chair of the Decentralization Task Force of the Initiative for Policy Dialogue at Columbia University. His research blends quantitative and qualitative methods to investigate the institutions and organizational forms that underpin rapid development. He has published extensively in the academic literature, including *Governance from Below: Decentralization and Popular Democracy in Bolivia* (University of Michigan Press), which won the W.J.M. Mackenzie Prize for best political science book of 2012. He also recently edited a special issue of *World Development* on "Decentralization and Governance" (2013), and co-edited *Descentralización y democratización en Bolivia: La historia del Estado débil, la sociedad rebelde y el anhelo de democracia* (with M. Zuazo and G. Bonifaz; Friedrich Ebert Stiftung, 2012). His teaching and research focus on comparative political economy, new institutional economics, economic development, and economic history. Faguet has a PhD from the London School of Economics, a master's degree from the JFK School at Harvard, and his bachelor's degree from Princeton University.

Christopher Gaukler is a consultant for the World Bank's Africa Social Protection Unit and has been working on Ethiopia since 2006. He focuses on monitoring and evaluation for the Basic Services team. Between 2011 and 2012, Gaukler worked as a monitoring and evaluation specialist for the government of South Sudan in the Ministry of Gender, Child, and Social Welfare. He has a master's degree from the School of Advanced International Studies at the Johns Hopkins University and an undergraduate degree from the University of Virginia.

Wendmsyamregne Mekasha (Wendm) is a Senior Social Protection Specialist in the World Bank office based in Addis Ababa, Ethiopia. He works on program monitoring and evaluation, building nationwide management information systems, and designing and implementing various analytical works including impact/process evaluation for programs and projects. Mekasha received his bachelor's degree in mathematics from Addis Ababa University (Ethiopia), his master's degree in agricultural economics from Haromaya University (Ethiopia), and his master's of liberal arts in general management from Harvard University (United States).

Executive Summary

Ethiopia, like most developing countries, has opted to deliver services such as basic education, primary health care, agricultural extension advice, water, and rural roads through a highly decentralized system (Manor 1999; Treisman 2007). That choice is based on several decades of theoretical analysis examining how a decentralized government might respond better to diverse local needs and provide public goods more efficiently than a highly centralized government.[1]

Ethiopia primarily manages the delivery of basic services at the *woreda* (district) level. Those services are financed predominantly through intergovernmental fiscal transfers (IGFTs) from the federal to the regional and then the woreda administrations, although some woredas raise a small amount of revenue to support local services. Since 2006, development partners and the government have cofinanced block grants for decentralized services through the Promoting Basic Services (PBS) Program. Aside from funding the delivery of services, the program supports measures to improve the quality of services and local governments' capacity to deliver them by strengthening accountability and citizen voice.[2]

Objectives

This study attempts to determine the extent to which spending at the woreda level on basic services is associated with key policy outputs and human outcomes. Woreda-level block grants primarily support locally recruited staff who provide basic services in five sectors (health, education, agriculture, water and sanitation, and rural roads). Because of limitations in the data, the analysis focuses on health, education, and agriculture. A parallel objective of the study is to assess the incidence of these expenditures by wealth quintile, in line with the World Bank's objective of achieving shared growth by reaching the bottom 40 percent. A final objective is to investigate whether the allocation of woreda-level block grants reflects the constitutional objective of providing additional resources to historically marginalized populations. In other words, how effective and equitable is spending on basic services at the woreda level? The study also looks at the effectiveness of efforts to improve financial transparency and accountability, social accountability, and grievance redress mechanisms, because of their strong influence on the availability and quality of basic services.

Overall Findings on the Effectiveness of a Decentralized Approach to Service Delivery

Ethiopia's model for delivering basic services appears to be succeeding and to confirm that services improve when service providers are more accountable to citizens. As discussed in the *World Development Report 2004* (World Bank 2003), accountability for delivering basic services can take an indirect, long route, in which citizens influence service providers through government, or a more direct, short route between service providers and citizens. When the long, indirect route of accountability is ineffective, service delivery can suffer, especially among poor or marginalized citizens who find it challenging to express their views to policy makers.

In Ethiopia, the indirect route of accountability works well precisely because of decentralization. Service providers are strictly accountable to local governments for producing results, but in turn, the local authorities are held accountable by the regional and federal governments. A degree of local competition for power and influence helps to induce local authorities and service provides to remain open to feedback from citizens and take responsibility for results. The direct route of accountability has been reinforced by measures to strengthen financial transparency and accountability (educating citizens on local budgets and publicly providing information on budgets and service delivery goals), social accountability (improving citizens' opportunities to provide feedback directly to local administrators and service providers), and impartial procedures to redress grievances (instituting the independent Ethiopian Institution of the Ombudsman, for example).

Woreda-level spending, financed through IGFTs and supported by the PBS Program, has been a very effective strategy for Ethiopia to attain its Millennium Development Goals (MDGs). Spending on health and education accounts for 80 percent of PBS-financed spending by the woredas, which goes to pay for health extension workers (HEWs) and teachers. Although the link between numbers of personnel hired and services delivered must be treated with caution (and is being explored in detail in another study), this study finds evidence that woreda-level spending in health and education is effective.

Owing to the intervention of HEWs, the use of health services has increased, especially among the poorest quintiles. Every additional US$1 of per capita spending by the woredas on health is associated with a 7.5 percent increase in the contraceptive prevalence rate and an 12.4 percent increase in deliveries by skilled birth attendants (Wang et al., forthcoming) (two interventions that can reduce maternal mortality dramatically), as well as a 4 percent increase in antenatal care (which can reduce infant and child mortality significantly). For education, an increase of US$1 per capita in spending by each woreda is associated with a 3.7 percent increase in the net primary enrollment rate within that woreda. Similar results are seen for the pupil-teacher ratio.

Finally, the effect of woreda-level spending on agricultural extension workers is associated with higher yields for major crops, including cereals, vegetables, enset, coffee, and fruit. Spending on agricultural extension workers increases the probability that farmers, regardless of the size of their plots, will use improved farming techniques.

Education, health, and agriculture account for 97 percent of woreda spending, which in turn constitutes 97 percent of PBS-financed IGFTs. This is complemented by support for greater engagement among citizens, improvements in local capacity to manage resources, and better access to information on national and local budgeting and development objectives. While it is difficult to provide precise estimates of the impact of the latter activities, the direction of their effect is clear: Spending efficiency is improved through better capacity, more transparency, and greater accountability to citizens.

In interpreting these results, it is important to bear in mind that the chain of causality from woreda spending to results is direct for education: Spending on teachers directly drives enrollments. For health and agriculture, on the other hand, spending at the woreda level on health and agricultural extension workers is best described as catalytic, because it increases the effectiveness of systemwide spending (federal capital investments in medical infrastructure, for example, or national research to develop improved varieties for farmers). Yet overall, these findings demonstrate the power of the PBS-financed decentralized approach for improving access to basic services, encouraging broadly shared development, and propelling Ethiopia rapidly toward the MDGs.

Improving Accountability and Citizen Voice in Providing Basic Services

The social accountability component of the PBS Program has increased the opportunities for constructive collaboration between citizens and the state to improve basic public services in pilot areas. Even though woredas must operate under federal guidelines, they still exercise a significant amount of discretion that can affect the quality of life and services. More than 84 percent of those surveyed in pilot areas responded positively to social accountability initiatives, which had increased citizens' awareness of their rights, responsibilities, and entitlements to basic services. After service providers and users drew up joint service improvement plans, basic services improved, and so did the quality of the engagement between citizens and service providers. Through the financial transparency and accountability component of the PBS Program, citizens have become more aware of the government budgeting process, and they are advocating more effectively for their rights as a result. The PBS Program has also improved the efficiency of resource use by improving financial management and procurement capacity at the woreda level.

Grievance redress mechanisms are another means of ensuring that citizens' voices are heard with respect to government services. A grievance redress mechanism provides the opportunity for an impartial third party to review a transaction that has taken place between the government and a citizen or a group of citizens. Through dialogue and technical and financial support, the PBS Program is strengthening the Ethiopian Institution of the Ombudsman and the regional Grievance Handling Offices, which offer these services.

Addressing Equity Issues in Providing Basic Services

Overall, the benefits of PBS-financed spending at the woreda level on health, education, and agriculture accrued to all income levels. Woreda-level spending on health and education is particularly pro-poor: 58 percent goes to the two bottom wealth quintiles.[3] In agriculture, woreda-level spending (primarily for agricultural extension workers) drives increases in output and the adoption of new, improved methods across all asset quintiles, although the magnitude was smaller for the bottom quintile, perhaps because of a lack of financing to purchase productivity-enhancing inputs.

Spending on basic services also appears to be reaching females, especially spending on health and education. In fact, health spending is undeniably pro-female, given that much of it promotes women's access to services that have a strong impact on reducing maternal mortality—including contraception, antenatal care, and assisted deliveries. Education is the only sector for which expenditure can be associated with data on results, disaggregated by gender, albeit for only two indicators—net enrollment rate and net intake rate at the primary level. The coefficient for female primary school students is slightly higher than for males for both net enrollment and intake, although not significant. The important finding is that no bias against females was found in expenditure on education, the sector that receives the bulk of PBS Program funds.

The results on agriculture tell a somewhat different and less clear story. Eighty-seven percent of Ethiopia's farmers are male, and access to extension services was found to favor males. It is not certain whether this bias is driven by gender differences in crop choices, the quality of land farmed by men compared to women, or some other inherent gender bias. Further analysis is required to clarify these issues and develop policy responses based on the evidence.

A final important question related to equity is whether PBS Program resources channeled to the woredas are reaching Ethiopia's historically disadvantaged regions and ethnic groups. The answer appears to be that in terms of basic service expenditure per capita, the current system broadly favors Ethiopia's historically disadvantaged regions compared to the historically dominant ones. More than 50 percent of the woredas in Gambella and 30 percent in Beneshangul-Gemuz—the two most disadvantaged regions of the country—spend more than 110 percent of the national average on the basic service sectors. Spending also appears to favor some historically disadvantaged ethnic groups, in accordance with constitutional mandates. Five majority-Anyiwak woredas are noteworthy for receiving the most public resources of all woredas in the nation. The exception occurs among the Somali groups. Federal transfers to Somali Region appear to be fine, but the region transfers a much smaller share to the woredas—49 percent, compared to the national average of 73 percent (excluding Addis Ababa) over the four years studied here.[4]

Conclusions and Recommendations

Decentralized spending at the woreda level is both effective and pro-poor. The estimates provided here imply that the returns to this spending are far from decreasing, which means that Ethiopia has scope to increase spending and speed its attainment of the MDGs.

The current approach also appears to be helping some of Ethiopia's historically disadvantaged areas and ethnic groups to catch up with the rest of the country. Expenditure to provide basic services at the woreda level is broadly equal across Ethiopia's woredas, with the striking exception of a small number of woredas that are concentrated in the country's most disadvantaged regions and receive significantly greater resources. Resource flows are lowest among the more developed, historically dominant regions.

In contrast to the predictions of some public management theories, the decentralized provision of services in Ethiopia is not increasing regional, ethnic, or gender inequalities in investment inputs or service outputs. Indeed, the opposite seems to be true for education and health, where the impact of PBS-financed IGFT resources was disproportionately high among the bottom two quintiles and women. In sum, support for decentralized services in Ethiopia appears to be an effective use of development partners' resources from both an efficiency and equity perspective.

The only exception to these findings is agriculture, for which the impact of PBS-financed IGFT expenditure was smaller for the bottom quintile. In this instance, a wide array of factors is likely to be at work, not the least of which could be poor farmers' inability to pay for productivity-enhancing inputs, land of poor quality, or water management issues that could not be controlled for in the analysis (except for rainfall).

Although quantitative evidence is unavailable at present, descriptive evidence from the first phase of the Ethiopia Social Accountability Program implies that structured feedback sessions involving citizens and service providers are strengthening citizens' participation in pilot areas. That evidence, together with the strong guidance emerging from governance and accountability theory, argues for the continued application of social accountability tools and the development of policies to sustain their use in the Ethiopian context. This conclusion can be verified when the impact assessment for the second phase of the Ethiopia Social Accountability Program becomes available.

The difficulty of conducting subnational empirical work on Ethiopia cannot be overstated. Creating the database for this study required considerable effort and improvisation on the part of the research team. The resulting standardized database of woreda-level expenditures and characteristics, which will be made public, is a major output of this study. The data will be augmented with new data collected under the third phase of the PBS Program and used in future research related to the program. It is hoped that in time this dataset will become a useful tool for researchers and students elsewhere in Africa and beyond.

Notes

1. See, for example, Tiebout (1956), Oates (1972), Besley and Coate (2003), and Faguet (2000, 2012).

2. The design of the PBS Program is influenced by the accountability triangle between government, service providers, and citizens (see World Bank 2003 and figure I.1 in the main text).

3. The Ethiopia section of an ongoing, multicountry study (Woldehanna, Tsehaye, and Hill, forthcoming) also finds that spending on primary education in Ethiopia (which is mostly managed by the woredas) is pro-poor—more so than overall spending on education (33 percent goes to the two bottom wealth quintiles).

4. Although spending at the woreda level in Somali Region appears to be lower than required to compensate for decades of underinvestment in basic services, the data for Somali woredas may be understated; some expenditures normally paid by woredas in other regions are paid regionally due to security and capacity constraints.

Abbreviations

AGSS	Agriculture Sample Survey
AIDS	acquired immune deficiency syndrome
ANC	antenatal care
CAR	contraceptive acceptance rate
CSA	Central Statistical Agency
DelSBA	deliveries by skilled birth attendants
DHS	Demographic and Health Survey
EFY	Ethiopia fiscal year
EIO	Ethiopian Institution of the Ombudsman
ETB	Ethiopian birr
FBG	Federal Block Grant
FTA	financial transparency and accountability
GDP	gross domestic product
HEW	health extension worker
HIV	human immunodeficiency virus
IDA	International Development Association
IGFT	intergovernmental fiscal transfer
MDG	Millennium Development Goal
NER	net enrollment rate
NIR	net intake rate
PBS	Promoting Basic Services (formerly, Protection of Basic Services) Program
PTR	pupil-teacher ratio
SNNP	Southern Nations, Nationalities, and Peoples (Region)
WASH	Water, Sanitation, and Hygiene
WBG	Woreda Block Grant

Introduction and Background

Among Ethiopia's recent impressive development results, its rapid improvement in basic service delivery indicators is outstanding. The Overseas Development Institute reports that Ethiopia has moved faster toward the Millennium Development Goals (MDGs) than *all but two other developing countries* (ODI 2010). According to the latest Ethiopia Demographic and Health Survey (DHS) data, child mortality fell from 123 per thousand in 2005 to 88 in 2010, and the primary net enrollment rate rose from 68 percent in 2004/05 to 82 percent in 2009/10.

Progress in delivering basic services over the past 10 years has been coupled with impressive economic growth: Gross development product (GDP) grew by 11 percent per annum on average between 2004/05 and 2009/10, according to official estimates. Initially led by agriculture, growth has become more broad based, with rising contributions from the mining, services, and manufacturing sectors. Ethiopia's growth may have slowed more recently, but it remains among the highest of any country in the world. The share of the population living in absolute poverty is declining as well: It fell from 38.7 percent in 2004/05 to 29.6 percent in 2011, according to official data.

All of these results spring from a long-term, concerted government commitment to pro-poor development. Building on the Sustainable Development and Poverty Reduction Program 2002–04/05 and the Plan for Accelerated and Sustained Development to End Poverty 2005–10, the government's current development plan, the Growth and Transformation Plan, aims to achieve the MDGs by 2015 and middle-income status for Ethiopia by 2020–23. Ethiopia achieved the MDG-4 (Child Mortality) target in 2014, ahead of schedule, and appears to be on track to reach the other MDGs by 2015, according to United Nations progress reports.

Under its constitution and legal framework, the government is committed to maintaining the integrity and capacity of the nation's decentralized administrations down to the woreda level.[1] Within Ethiopia's federal structure, the central government provides unearmarked block grants through regional governments, which in turn provide block grants to woreda administrations to deliver services to citizens. This administrative and financial structure has provided timely, predictable financing to support a steady and impressive increase in basic services throughout the country. But has Ethiopia's decentralized approach to delivering basic services been cost effective?

For decades, analysts have debated whether decentralization can make government more responsive to diverse local needs and more efficient in providing public goods.[2] The job of providing basic services generally falls to local governments, so building their capacity is an important part of improving basic services. For shared growth and development to occur, it is vital that such services reach the poorest 40 percent of the population. Ethiopia's fiscal architecture makes it a rich, promising empirical setting for investigating the effectiveness of decentralization as a tool for improving both the quality and distribution of public sector outputs. The evidence that Ethiopia can offer is especially welcome because so much of the empirical evidence that has accumulated on decentralization over the past four decades has been inconclusive.

Consider the evidence from the broadest empirical surveys. Rondinelli, Cheema, and Nellis (1983) note that decentralization has usually disappointed its advocates. Most developing countries have encountered serious administrative problems in implementing decentralization. The few comprehensive evaluations that have been conducted of the costs and benefits of decentralization report limited success in some countries but none in others. A decade and a half later, surveys by Piriou-Sall (1998), Manor (1999), and Smoke (2001) were slightly more positive but contained caveats about the strength of the evidence in favor of decentralization. Manor notes that the evidence, though extensive, is incomplete, but concludes that "while decentralization…is no panacea, it has many virtues and is worth pursuing." Smoke, by contrast, finds the evidence mixed and anecdotal, and asks whether there is any empirical justification for pursuing decentralization. Given the sheer size of the literature, the lack of progress toward an overarching conclusion is surprising.

It is worth noting that more recent empirical studies, which are often technically more sophisticated thanks to the enormous improvement in data from developing countries over recent decades, are generally more positive about decentralization's potential. At least five recent studies address the link between decentralization and substantive outcomes directly and with rigorous quantitative evidence. Escaleras and Register (2012) find that fiscal decentralization is associated with lower natural disaster death rates, implying more effective preparation and/or responses to natural disasters by countries with decentralized governments. Clark (2009) applies regression discontinuity to a natural experiment from Great Britain and concludes that schools opting out of the centralized education regime—in effect decentralizing themselves—enjoy large increases in student achievement. Galiani, Gertler, and Schargrodsky (2008) find that moving the control of schools from central to provincial governments in Argentina had a positive impact on students' test scores. The poorest, however, did not gain from decentralization and indeed may have lost. Barankay and Lockwood (2007) report that greater decentralization of education to Swiss cantons is associated with higher educational attainment, especially for boys. By adding empirical evidence from Ethiopia, a low-income country where large programs in decentralization and public investment are yielding potentially significant results, this study makes an important contribution to the literature.

Context and Structure of This Book

This book is based on a report issued as part of a programmatic knowledge series for Ethiopia on improving services for the poorest citizens.[3] Future reports will elucidate the findings presented here in several ways. For example, they will present the results of additional studies of the quality of service delivery in health and education, drawing on data from ongoing surveys; offer a detailed assessment of the impact of the Promoting Basic Services (PBS) Program, based on multiround surveys over the next three years; and assess the impact of the social accountability component of PBS (the baseline survey is complete, and a full report is due in two years). The findings reported here will be updated next year, when results from the mini Demographic and Health Survey (DHS) are available, but they are being issued now to provide input into the government's next Growth and Transformation Plan.

This book begins by describing the PBS Program and detailing how intergovernmental fiscal transfers (IGFTs) are channeled through Ethiopia's decentralized federal structure to support the provision of basic services. The sections that follow focus on the approach used for the analysis, along with the governance and accountability mechanisms that are integral to the PBS Program. Findings on the effectiveness of local spending (IGFTs) for achieving development results in education, health, and agriculture are reported in detail. Subsequent sections examine the equity impacts of the PBS Program with respect to income, gender, and historically disadvantaged regions and ethnic groups. The book concludes with a summary of the results and a series of recommendations. Four appendixes provide additional details on the methodology and context for the study.

The Promoting Basic Services Program

Through the PBS Program, the Government of Ethiopia and development partners cofinance block grants to support the provision of basic services at the local level (the government's share of the financing is larger and rising). The block grants are distributed from the federal government to the regional governments using a formula that adjusts for the size of the population in each region and for need, based on the current level of development and historic lack of access to services. The funds are transmitted from the regions to the woredas using regional formulas based on similar criteria.

Aside from providing block grants to woredas, the PBS Program supports various measures designed to improve the quality of basic services and local governments' capacity to manage them. The program's design is influenced by the concept of the "accountability triangle" between policy makers, citizens, and service providers, described in the *World Development Report 2004: Making Services Work for Poor People* (figure I.1). The program's design recognizes that the long "indirect route" of accountability, in which citizens appeal to policy makers (government) to hold service providers to account, must be complemented by a shorter "direct route," in which citizens can directly hold service providers accountable for results.

In Ethiopia, the indirect route of accountability works well precisely because of decentralization (box I.1). Service providers are strictly accountable to local governments for producing results, but, in turn, the local authorities are held accountable by the regional and federal governments for delivering basic services and reaching the delivery targets set in the Growth and Transformation Plan. The teachers, health workers, and agricultural extension workers

Figure I.1 The Triangle of Accountability in Service Delivery

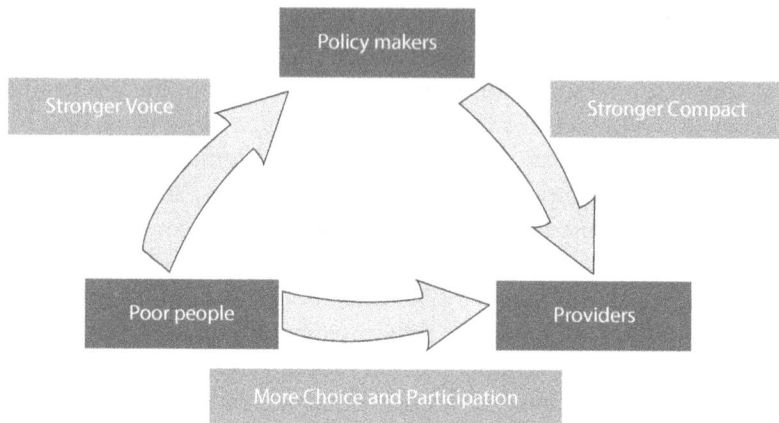

Source: World Bank 2003.

who deliver those services are recruited and managed by the woreda leadership. Local competition for these leadership positions is significant, and officeholders are keen to reach their service delivery targets. This arrangement encourages local authorities to listen to citizens and take responsibility for results. On the other hand, the direct route of accountability is reinforced by measures that strengthen financial transparency and accountability (educating citizens on local budgets and service delivery goals), social accountability (improving citizens' opportunities to provide feedback directly to local administrators and service providers), and impartial procedures to redress grievances (instituting the independent Ethiopian Institution of the Ombudsman, for example).

Recognizing the critical role of good information to improve development outcomes, the PBS Program also finances a range of surveys and other data collection and management efforts. Capacity building includes training in financial management and procurement for local woredas, in addition to other types of training, based on demand.

Woreda-level block grants primarily support locally recruited staff in five decentralized sectors (education, health, agriculture, water and sanitation, and rural roads). With some minor exceptions, woredas have very little revenue of their own, and they receive no other regular and predictable transfers that can be used to support staff. For that reason, total woreda spending in sectors relevant to the PBS Program is used here as a proxy for the block grants cofinanced by PBS partners and the government. Health sector spending focuses on health extension workers (HEWs), education spending on teachers, agriculture spending on agricultural extension workers (also referred to as development agents), water sector spending on recurrent costs for water systems, and road spending on road maintenance staff. In health, education, and agriculture there is a one-to-one correlation between woreda-level block grant spending and HEWs, teachers, and agricultural extension workers.

Box I.1 The Indirect Route of Accountability Through Policy Makers to Service Providers

In Ethiopia's strong push to achieve middle-income status by the mid-2020s, the federal, regional, and woreda governments all assign high priority to attaining development results quickly, especially in the basic service sectors. The Ethiopian state has high expectations of performance from civil service staff at the decentralized levels of government. These individuals, who are responsible for moving their communities toward specific development outcomes, are at the heart of the relationship between policy makers and service providers.

Policymakers operating at the local level are held accountable to their higher-ups, and the Ethiopian government expects officials at every level to deliver results. The accountability between policy makers and service providers is one of the three sides of the "accountability triangle" depicted in the *World Development Report 2004*. Policy makers have some degree of control over providers' results, and well-intentioned policy makers can put into place the appropriate mechanisms and incentives to drive positive outcomes.

Two elements of Ethiopia's system influence the degree of accountability and deserve note. First, decentralization has created woreda offices that are positions of inherent prestige, conferring a certain level of power and influence in the community. To some extent, competition for these desirable positions leads local authorities to feel responsible for results and to remain open to feedback from citizens. Second, the relationship between local policy makers, service providers, and the community is strengthened by recruiting individuals locally: Teachers, health workers, and other local residents hired to provide services are apt to feel an intrinsic motivation to serve their community.

According the *World Development Report 2004*, "a critical element in the policymaker-provider relationship is information." A woreda's improvements in the enrollment rate or the provision of antenatal care, for example, create an impression of the relative success or failure of the woreda's officials. Similarly, knowledge of provider absenteeism enables woreda officials to hold specific service providers to account. The financial transparency and social accountability components of the PBS Program, as well as efforts to strengthen monitoring, evaluation, and related reporting from each sector, are providing additional opportunities to improve the accountability of service providers.

The PBS Program is the primary means by which the World Bank and other development partners assist Ethiopia to achieve the MDGs. At the program's inception in 2006, Ethiopia had just started to register noticeable improvements in human development indicators, albeit from low absolute levels. The Project Appraisal Document for the first phase of PBS clearly stated the challenge of maintaining that nascent progress in the face of political and economic uncertainty: "These gains represent the first steps on a steep development trajectory that Ethiopia will need to sustain if it is to have a chance to meet any of the MDGs" (World Bank 2012a). Eight years on, it is obvious that through the PBS Program, Ethiopia is meeting that challenge, and more. The current five-year third phase of PBS costs US$6.4 billion, of which about half is financed by the government.

Table I.1 shows the evolution of Federal Block Grants (FBGs) provided to the regions by the federal government between 2005/06 and 2012/13; Table I.2 shows the evolution of Woreda Block Grants (WBGs) provided by the regions to the woredas.

While helping to achieve many of the eight MDGs, the PBS Program focuses principally on three—achieving universal primary school education (Goal 2), reducing child mortality (Goal 4), and improving maternal health (Goal 5)—and also has a direct impact on the eradication of extreme poverty and hunger (Goal 1) and the promotion of gender equality (Goal 3). The program takes advantage of Ethiopia's well-developed system of fiscal decentralization, which was well under way when the program began, to channel resources to the

Table I.1 Federal Block Grants and PBS Program Disbursements

	2005/06	2006/07	2007/08	2008/09	2009/10	2010/11	2011/12	2012/13
Federal Block Grants (FBGs) to the regions (ETB million)	7,071.5	9,365.0	13,532.5	16,554.8	19,555.7	25,555.8	30,576.4	35,555.3
Federal government expenditures (Treasury source only) (ETB million)	21,856.5	26,976.2	34,717.4	41,053.8	53,063.7	67,769.6	83,470.2	89,064.2
FBGs as a share of federal government expenditures	*32.4*	*34.7*	*39.0*	*40.3*	*36.9*	*37.7*	*36.6*	*39.9*
PBS donors' contribution to FBGs (US$ million)	91.0	446.7	477.9	437.2	453.9	542.6	329.5	444.5
Average exchange rate (ETB/US$)	8.6810	8.7943	9.2441	10.4205	12.8909	16.1081	17.7686	18.1947
PBS donors' contribution to FBGs (ETB million)	790.0	3,928.8	4,417.7	4,556.3	5,851.7	8,741.0	5,855.1	8,087.4
PBS donors' contribution to FBGs (%)	*11.2*	*42.0*	*32.6*	*27.5*	*29.9*	*34.2*	*19.1*	*22.7*
IDA's contribution to FBGs (%)	*11.2*	*9.4*	*12.4*	*14.7*	*14.8*	*12.9*	*12.1*	*9.5*
FBGs as a share of total regional expenditures	*76.2*	*88.5*	*85.3*	*86.2*	*79.8*	*80.4*	*62.8*	*54.4*

Source: Ministry of Finance and Economic Development for the data on FBGs and federal government expenditures, PBS donors for data on PBS disbursements, and National Bank of Ethiopia for exchange rate data.
Note: ETB = Ethiopian birr; IDA = International Development Association; PBS = Promoting Basic Services.

Table I.2 Total Woreda Recurrent Expenditures by Region

ETB million

Region	2005/06	2006/07	2007/08	2008/09	2009/10	2010/11	2011/12	2012/13
Tigray	457.3	556.9	797.6	941.9	1,040.0	1,426.7	1,837.8	2,265.0
Afar	126.9	119.2	191.2	247.9	278.3	371.3	405.5	481.4
Amhara	1,385.4	1,363.1	2,160.2	2,956.2	3,136.5	3,787.2	5,522.7	6,429.4
Oromia	2,056.7	2,109.8	3,070.7	4,312.9	4,401.9	5,866.5	6,957.0	8,887.9
Somali	217.8	232.0	367.2	282.0	459.3	626.9	972.3	1,123.0
Beneshangul-Gemuz	100.3	124.1	148.2	167.1	216.7	293.1	452.7	488.7
SNNP	1,250.4	1,539.2	1,910.1	2,097.9	3,012.6	3,950.5	5,161.1	6,279.5
Gambella	69.4	84.2	127.8	140.1	151.3	202.1	286.9	351.0
Harari	0.0	24.2	24.2	33.9	38.3	48.8	60.1	73.7
Dire Dawa	0.0	14.4	27.8	28.3	31.7	31.8	41.4	52.2
Addis Ababa	507.2	534.9	656.9	1,187.0	1,178.9	1,447.3	1,922.9	2,581.0
All regions	6,171.3	6,702.2	9,481.8	12,395.1	13,945.3	18,052.0	23,620.3	29,012.9
All regions (excluding Addis Ababa)	5,664.1	6,167.3	8,825.0	11,208.1	12,766.5	16,604.8	21,697.4	26,431.8

Source: World Bank based on Ministry of Finance and Economic Development data.

woreda level to finance recurrent expenditures and efficiently deliver and expand services in the five sectors mentioned earlier. At the local level, this funding is used to deploy frontline development workers and in this sense is linked to meeting MDG targets. HEWs, for example, promote preventive behaviors and provide basic health interventions, such as vaccinations and family planning information, which serve to reduce child mortality and improve maternal health. The hiring of additional teachers is related directly to increasing net enrollment rates in order to achieve universal primary education. Funds transferred to the woredas in the first two phases of the PBS Program helped to hire more than 100,000 new primary school teachers, 38,000 HEWs, and 45,000 agricultural extension agents, dramatically expanding access to their respective services.

Despite the impressive scale of the PBS Program, prior to this study no empirical analysis was done to assess the effects of PBS spending on outcomes, partly because of the difficulty of obtaining data on local expenditures and outcomes over time. One of this study's signal accomplishments is that it has compiled comprehensive expenditure data through time and consolidated it into a database with output indicators for health and education for the same time period—a prerequisite for the analysis that follows.

Notes

1. Appendix C briefly describes the evolution of the modern Ethiopian Federal State.

2. See, for example, Tiebout (1956), Oates (1972), Besley and Coate (2003), and Faguet (2000, 2012).

3. World Bank (2014). This programmatic knowledge series complements another programmatic knowledge series in Ethiopia, led by the Poverty Reduction Economic Management network, which will include a poverty assessment, public expenditure reviews, and various reports on growth and employment.

CHAPTER 1

Conceptual Framework and Methodology

A primary objective of this study is to assess the relationship between expenditure at the woreda level to provide basic services in five sectors and *key outputs and outcomes* for those sectors, focusing particularly on health, education, and agriculture (for which the best data are available).[1] As noted, woreda-level spending in those three sectors is associated strongly with key service *outputs*, such as numbers of teachers, health extension workers (HEWs), and agricultural extension workers.

This study focuses on such *outcomes* as the net enrollment rate, rates of vaccination and contraceptive use, and agricultural yields of a variety of crops (see figure 1.1 for a diagrammatic representation of the Promoting Basic Services [PBS] results chain). An important consideration is that the link between

Figure 1.1 Conceptual Model of the Results Chain of PBS Spending

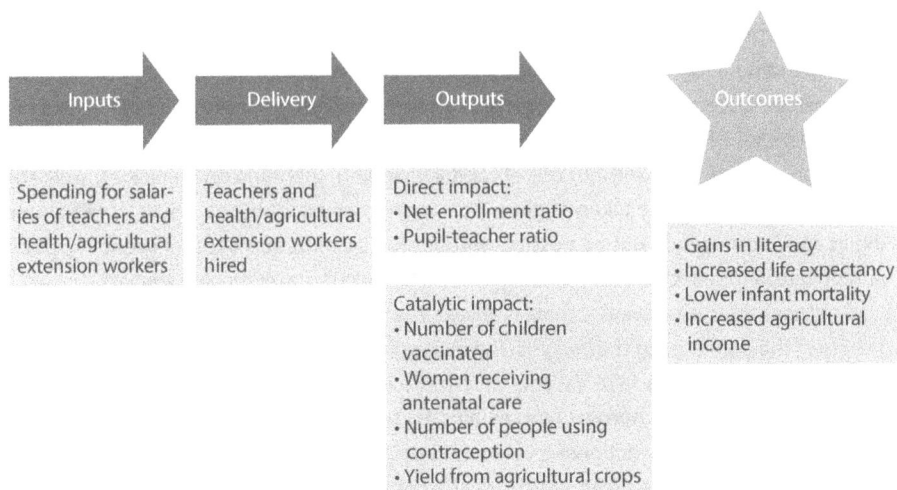

Inputs	Delivery	Outputs	Outcomes
Spending for salaries of teachers and health/agricultural extension workers	Teachers and health/agricultural extension workers hired	Direct impact: • Net enrollment ratio • Pupil-teacher ratio Catalytic impact: • Number of children vaccinated • Women receiving antenatal care • Number of people using contraception • Yield from agricultural crops	• Gains in literacy • Increased life expectancy • Lower infant mortality • Increased agricultural income

spending on staff and results cannot be one to one; service availability and use need to be assessed as well. Unfortunately such data are not available for the most part, with the very limited exception of the health sector, where Demographic and Health Survey (DHS) data show that the use of health services, especially by the poor, is catalyzed by HEWs (Wang et al., forthcoming). Other caveats concern the quality of the data and local effects of spending outside the PBS Program (box 1.1).

A parallel objective of this study is to assess the incidence of local expenditures by wealth quintile, in line with the World Bank's objective of achieving shared growth by targeting the bottom 40 percent. Another objective is to investigate the allocation of block grants at the woreda level in relation to Ethiopia's constitutional objective of providing additional resources to historically underserved ethnic groups. A final objective, related to the triangle of accountability shown in figure I.1, is to assess the components of the PBS Program that are designed to strengthen citizen voice in improving basic services.

This study makes use of a database comprising woreda-level recurrent expenditures and information on outcomes for a variety of health and education indicators at the woreda level between 2008 and 2011. These data are complemented by Agriculture Sample Survey (AGSS) data and information from the 2007 census on the demographic characteristics of each woreda, including its overall

---

Box 1.1 Some Caveats on Interpreting the Results of This Study

Please note that while the results reported in the text are for log-linear regressions, we also estimated quadratic and linear regressions in addition to probits. The detailed results are in appendix D.

Clearly, the local development results achieved in the sectors studied here are affected by spending from other levels of government, such as capital spending and nonsalary recurrent costs. Examples include the cost of learning materials (financed separately in education) and the costs of facilities above the health center level (financed separately in health). PBS Program spending in agriculture and roads includes only spending on extension workers and road maintenance staff. In other words, it is important to keep in mind that the results presented here for PBS spending—in health, for example—show the catalytic effect of health extension workers; the contributions of capital spending, spending on medicines, and other types of expenditures are taken as given. To cite another example, the results of PBS spending in agriculture would not be possible without the contribution of other spending, public and private, and reflect only the catalytic effects of agricultural extension workers.

Another important caveat is that, as always, the results presented here are subject to the quality of the data used in the analysis. The management information systems for health and especially education are fairly reliable and improving (not least through PBS support), although much room for improvement remains. Fortunately, the results for health and education can be confirmed by national-level analysis of DHS data. The analysis for agriculture uses Agriculture Sample Survey data, which are also considered reliable.

---

population, ethnic composition, the percentage of the population that is rural and urban, and other variables. Econometric modeling is used to assess the association of increased local spending with the expansion of basic services and outcomes, and by extension the efficiency of the PBS Program in meeting its development objective. The study also verifies the woreda-level findings in health and education using the household data from DHS 2005 and 2011, including the use of limited dependent variable (primarily probit) regressions to predict the impact on household behavior of interactions with HEWs.

Cross-time pooled regressions with the log of the outcome variable of interest on the left-hand side were run to evaluate the result of the log per capita sector expenditure, controlling for shares of rural/urban population and ethnicity (which constitute a good proxy for historical lags in development). A variable for time was included to isolate the time-series effects from other effects. The main text presents results from the log-linear regressions, which are preferred because they eliminate the effects of extreme values and allow for declining returns to scale. Linear regressions and quadratic regressions were also estimated (see appendix A).

The indicators evaluated are drawn mostly from the PBS Results Framework. No reliable data on outcomes at the woreda level were available for agriculture, water supply, and roads, so alternative approaches were used. For agriculture, zonal data on outcomes were available to assess the effectiveness of spending on agriculture, taking the average per capita woreda spending on agriculture as a proxy for services offered by agricultural extension workers. More severe data constraints for water supply and roads made it necessary to resort to desk reviews.[2]

Conducting subnational empirical work on Ethiopia involves numerous challenges and constraints. Relatively little data is collected, the data are often of poor quality, and few attempts are made to systematize the results into any obviously comparable framework. A few illustrations are telling. Until very recently, fiscal data on subnational expenditures in health, education, agriculture, water, and roads were available only for Ethiopia Fiscal Year (EFY) 2003. Their geographic identifying codes and names do not match those used for census data, in which geographic codes and names vary in unpredictable but pervasive ways from fiscal data. The last census counted some 740 woredas, zones, and regions, but the fiscal dataset includes more than 850. Consolidating these two sources yielded a dataset of 989 subnational units, 250 more than in the census.

The analysis consists of three key stages. Stage I follows the approach of Faguet (2012) and Faguet and Sánchez (2013), examining the relationship between woreda-level spending in each sector (figure 1.2) and results in those sectors. Ideally first differences would be used on the outcome left-hand-side variables, but the few years of data currently available make this procedure impractical. Instead, trends are estimated by placing levels on the left-hand side.

Stage II is an incidence analysis of woreda-level spending by quintile, using the wealth quintile breakdown from the DHS survey. Improvements in health and education outcomes are allocated to each quintile by pro-rating the expenditure increases to each quintile by the improvement in outcomes achieved for that

Figure 1.2 Woreda-Level Expenditure in the Five PBS Sectors, 2011

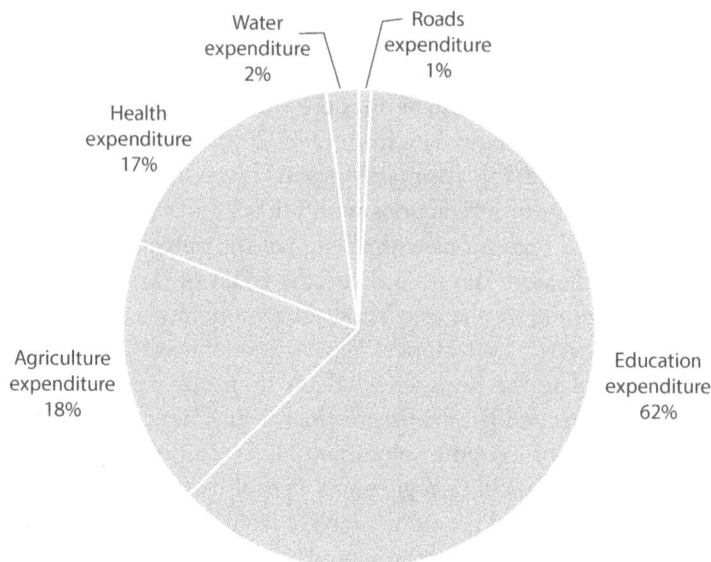

Water expenditure 2%
Roads expenditure 1%
Health expenditure 17%
Agriculture expenditure 18%
Education expenditure 62%

Source: World Bank calculations using data collected from regional and Woreda bureaus of the Ministry of Finance and Economic Development.

quintile, controlling for the average improvement for all groups.[3] The results indicator for education was the net enrollment rate, which is directly affected by the number of teachers recruited for the woreda. For health, the results indicator is an average of four indicators that are affected directly by locally recruited HEWs: increased use of contraception, increased rates of immunization, increased use of antenatal care, and increased use of skilled birth attendants.

In stage III, limited dependent variable regressions are used to examine the link between woreda expenditure and sectoral results for different wealth quintiles[4] to estimate probabilities that households will act in a certain manner. This three-stage analysis was limited to sectors with reliable data on woreda-level results and corresponding household survey data on health and education.

For education, the third-stage test was considered unnecessary because of the direct linkage between woreda-level spending, which is mostly for teachers, and the net enrollment rate. The third-stage test was needed for health, however, because the linkage between spending on HEWs and results is less direct. In that case, the link between contact with HEWs and health sector outcomes was tested using DHS data.

Given that no output data were available for agriculture at the woreda level, the effect of agricultural extension services was analyzed by plot-size quintile. No national or local analysis could be done for water supply; a recent national census found that the data were unreliable, and in any event the sector accounts for only 2 percent of woreda-level expenditure. Nor was in-depth analysis possible for roads (which account for only 1 percent of woreda-level expenditure).

Notes

1. Note that this study does not look at the quality or effectiveness of service delivery, however. Phase three of the PBS Program supports the collection of data on service delivery indicators for health and education, which will be used in future studies of those issues.

2. Normally, DHS has good water supply data, but definitional changes between the two rounds of DHS in Ethiopia have made the water supply data incompatible.

3. This methodology was adopted because there were no data on direct use of different services by quintile. This approach assumes a link between woreda-recruited staff and results.

4. Education and health quintiles were based on DHS quintiles. Quintile estimates for agriculture used land-size quintiles.

CHAPTER 2

Citizen Direct Voice and Accountability

Before discussing the effectiveness and equity analyses of woreda-level spending to provide basic services, it is important to document how the context of accountability is changing in Ethiopia with respect to service provision. Mechanisms that enhance financial transparency, increase social accountability, and permit grievances to be addressed all strengthen citizens' capacity to share their concerns effectively with service providers and local authorities (box 2.1). Note that one element of direct accountability that is not common in Ethiopia outside larger urban centers is the market for basic services, because private providers are concentrated in major centers.

Box 2.1 The Direct Route of Accountability—Citizen Direct Voice and Accountability Models in Ethiopia

Decentralization brings service providers under the control of local governments and their constituents.[a] Staffing levels and allocations are centrally approved, but personnel are locally hired and managed—and in theory more directly accountable to the community. For accountability to occur, however, local residents must be able to understand the issues surrounding service delivery and the options for voicing their concerns. The Promoting Basic Services (PBS) Program is testing and in some cases scaling up complementary strategies to strengthen citizens' voice and access to information.

For example, the project's **financial transparency and accountability** component makes information about local government budgets and spending publicly available in a simple, clear format. Through budget literacy training, citizens learn how to provide feedback to local authorities on budgets and the provision of basic services.

The project's **social accountability** component uses structured social accountability tools such as community score cards, citizen report cards, participatory budgeting, and interface (direct) meetings between service providers and service users to make services better, more accessible, and more effective. These tools are being used in more than 340 woredas by about 4.5 million service users. A rigorous, independent evaluation based on a randomized

box continues next page

Box 2.1 The Direct Route of Accountability—Citizen Direct Voice and Accountability Models in Ethiopia *(continued)*

controlled trial is under way to examine the impact of these tools and determine whether they should be made available nationally.

The project also plans to strengthen and expand the use of **grievance redress mechanisms.** A grievance redress mechanism provides the opportunity for an impartial third party to review a transaction that has taken place between the government and a citizen or a group of citizens, who assert that a government service or benefit has been denied, or some other harm has occurred. The Ethiopian Institution of the Ombudsman (EIO) and the regional Grievance Handling Offices offer these services. The EIO is an independent entity that has six regional branches and is accountable to the Federal Parliament. Grievance Handling Offices, established in all nine regional states, examine the validity of citizens' grievances and find ways to rectify them. They are accountable to the respective chief administrator in their regional state and receive technical support and capacity building from the EIO.

a. See Faguet (2004) for an in-depth discussion of the theory surrounding this topic, and Faguet and Wietzke (2006) for practical applications.

Decentralization and the Quality and Appropriateness of Local Services

Until woreda-level data from the period before decentralization are available, it will not be possible to estimate the effects of decentralization *per se* (in the sense of the transfer of expenditure and decision-making authority from upper to lower tiers of government) on financial flows, service provision, or substantive outcomes. These are the questions on which the decentralization literature typically focuses, and when data permit, they will be addressed in future reports.

Other, more micro-level questions can be examined with the data assembled for this study, however. They concern the effects of woreda-level discretion and decision making on the quality of services and their appropriateness to local conditions. These questions are distinct from "big discretion" issues, such as how to divide resources between investment and expenditure, or how to allocate spending between schools, hospitals, and roads. "Small discretion" questions concern such issues as how to target a vaccination campaign, or when and exactly how to maintain a road, or which side of a road or stream is the best location for a new school. Decisions of this kind, which can increase the efficiency and reduce the cost of public services by tailoring services to highly specific local conditions and needs, are the bread and butter of local governments.

Small discretion has other important effects on service delivery. Centrally established staffing norms determine the local funding available for particular sectors, but the actual hiring of staff occurs at the woreda level. Local hiring can influence the attendance of teachers, health extension workers (HEWs), and agricultural extension workers, because the hiring and paying authority is present in the immediate area where they work. Absenteeism is near 50 percent in many countries that centrally recruit and deploy teachers. The limited evidence available for Ethiopia shows that teacher absenteeism is about 15 percent.[1] The same study finds that only 10.4 percent of respondents said that health staff were frequently absent, including the HEWs who serve the immediate community. Nearly all respondents (96 percent) reported that agricultural extension workers were present in their *kebele* (subdistrict), and 95 percent found them to be useful. This is the effect of small discretion. More services are delivered because more service providers are on the job, and if they are not, evidence indicates that a significant percentage of citizens will complain to their local government about it (Kamurase and Alibhai 2014). In sum, the limited data show that decentralization increases accountability, and that even if a small number of citizens make their voices heard, they can have a positive effect on the quality of service delivery.

Ethiopia's decentralization law also allows citizens from different ethnic or language groups to request their own woreda and education in their own language. Such actions appear bound to introduce a greater measure of local accountability and increase learning effectiveness.

Financial Transparency and Accountability

Over the last five years, financial transparency and accountability (FTA) tools designed under the PBS Program have been rolled out to disclose information on regional and local budgets, service delivery targets, and accomplishments. More than 90 percent of Ethiopia's woredas and city administrations now post such information publicly. Aside from posting information, regions also use radio and television programs, brochures, t-shirts, and other means to disseminate information. These actions have revolutionized transparency, as this key information was not released to the public before 2006.

The increase in transparency has not been even across the country. A recent survey (Selam Development Consultants 2013, 34–35) finds that 42.5 percent of respondents have seen FTA templates posted in their jurisdictions. It is encouraging that citizens are not merely passively receiving this information but are responding to it. More than 230,000 citizens across all woredas and city administrations have received budget literacy training to improve their understanding of the budget process and service delivery issues. As a result, over time more citizens are discussing budget and spending priorities with their local officials, providing feedback on budget execution, and monitoring project implementation. The survey mentioned earlier finds that 37 percent of respondents have discussed budget information with their woreda or city officials. Another 26 percent have discussed the information with other citizens. Nor is this communication one sided. Some 37 percent of survey respondents indicated that woreda and city officials had sought citizens' views on budgetary issues, and 43 percent revealed that officials had also sought citizens' views on the quality of public services. (See appendix B for more detail.)

Social Accountability

The social accountability component of the PBS Program complements FTA initiatives by supporting civil society organizations and other means for citizens to provide feedback to local administrators and service providers.[2] In an earlier phase of PBS, 86 woredas tested tools such as community score cards, citizen report cards, and participatory budgeting. They also promoted interface meetings between citizens and local authorities to provide feedback on service delivery.

Following a positive evaluation of those pilot efforts, the current phase of PBS features an expanded social accountability component.[3] The evaluation finds that more than 84 percent of the individuals surveyed in pilot areas responded positively to social accountability initiatives, which had increased citizens' awareness of their rights, responsibilities, and entitlements to basic services. After service providers and users drew up joint service improvement plans, basic services improved, and so did the quality of the engagement between citizens and service providers. These findings bear out the prediction of the model shown in figure I.1.

During the current phase of the PBS Program, participating woredas are continuing to use the tools piloted in the first phase. Interface meetings between users and providers of services, along with woreda and kebele officials, continue as well, in addition to the development of agreed joint action plans monitored by joint committees of service users and providers. In 224 woredas, 49 Social Accountability Implementing Partners are working to assist public service providers to deliver better-quality services in education, health, agriculture, water and sanitation, and rural roads, in response to feedback from communities and citizen groups. Other social accountability tools will be considered carefully, based on their value added, including participatory planning and budgeting, budget tracking, gender-responsive budgeting, and service charters. (See appendix B for details.)

The government is exploring strategies to sustain and strengthen these social accountability initiatives. Initial thoughts on such a policy highlight the need to strengthen linkages and synergies between social accountability and FTA, evaluate the implementation of recommendations on linkages, and develop more medium- and long-term options based on those evaluations.

Grievance Redress Mechanisms

A study conducted under the auspices of the PBS Program in 2011 determined that Ethiopia had established several grievance redress mechanisms in different regions under various programs (Randolph and Edjeta 2011). The mechanisms varied significantly in their legal underpinnings, procedures, the government entity to which they were responsible, accountability, and the finality and enforcement of grievance findings.

Through dialogue and technical and financial support, the PBS Program aims to strengthen the Grievance Handling Offices at the regional state level by improving public awareness of the services they provide, delivering technical assistance to develop a common standard of grievance redress procedures, and developing the capacity of grievance handling officers. The PBS Program also supports the opening of Grievance Handling Offices in all regional states, as well as branches of the Ethiopian Institution of the Ombudsman (EIO). Currently the PBS Program finances capacity building and training workshops conducted by EIO for regional EIO branch offices and regional grievance handling officers. It also supports studies to aid in standardizing and improving the grievance redress system across the country. This important contribution supports and expands the forums where ordinary citizens can air their concerns.

Notes

1. Based on initial results from a baseline survey conducted for an assessment of the social accountability component of the PBS Program. Data on absenteeism include not just absence from school but also absence from the classroom. See Kamurase and Alibhai (2014).
2. Under PBS, social accountability activities are financed through a programmatic multidonor trust fund administered by the International Development Association (IDA), though without IDA resources.
3. IPE Global (2010). The assessment was not a formal evaluation but relied more on recapitulative data. As mentioned, the new phase of PBS was designed to include a full, rigorous evaluation, for which a baseline survey has been completed.

CHAPTER 3

Effectiveness of Woreda Block Grant Spending on Education, Health, and Agriculture

A Positive Association between Woreda Block Spending and Results in Education

Over half of the resources channeled to local governments under the Promoting Basic Services (PBS) Program are used to hire primary school teachers.[1] Demographic and Health Survey (DHS) data indicate that the net enrollment rate for primary school climbed from 68 percent to 82 percent between 2005 and 2011, and the completion rate rose from 34 to 49 percent. The analysis that follows sought to determine if there was an association between per capita expenditures on primary education at the woreda level and the net enrollment rate (NER) and pupil-teacher ratio (PTR). The third phase of the PBS Program is expected to achieve specific improvements in both of these education-related indicators, which are included in the results framework.

The analysis did not consider nonsalary recurrent costs in education, which are covered by other levels of government.[2] The exclusion of those costs is not expected to affect the results of the analysis to a great extent, given that teacher costs constitute more than 90 percent of recurrent costs in basic education. The model does consider the impact of capital costs such as school buildings, however, which can drive enrollments. Capital expenditure is based on per capita expenditures at the regional level, where most capital spending occurs. Table 3.1 presents the main coefficients of interest from the log-linear regression analysis.

Both net enrollment rate and pupil-teacher ratio show a strong and significant relationship with woreda-level per capita recurrent expenditure, after controlling for the effects of rural/urban percentage and ethnicity. For every additional Ethiopian birr (ETB) per capita of woreda education spending, net enrollment rate increases by 0.20 percent. These results are all significant at the 1 percent level and robust to changes in specification. The results for pupil-teacher ratio are similar.

Table 3.1 Association of Log of Per Capita Education Expenditure with Log of Education Outcomes

Independent variable	Dependent variable/indicator	Coefficient/(SE)	Significance
Log of expenditure	Log of net enrollment rate	0.2757 (.0280)	***
	Log of pupil-teacher ratio	−0.2229 (.0203)	***

Source: Based on Poverty and Social Impact Analysis Database from 2008 to 2011.
Note: Number of observations is 2,583 for NER and 2,695 for PTR. Standard errors given in parentheses; *** indicates significance at 1 percent level.

A Positive Association between Woreda Block Grant Spending and Results in Health

About 20 percent of PBS Program resources channeled to the local level are used in the health sector, mainly to hire frontline health extension workers (HEWs) (box 3.1). HEWs do not provide extensive curative services; their assignment is to support public health in several important ways. They promote healthy lifestyle practices in the community and refer complicated cases, such as difficult pregnancies or severe child malnutrition, to a health center, where they can be treated by health professionals with more extensive training. They also provide services that can be scheduled periodically, the most important being immunizations, family planning (insertion of contraceptive implants), and antenatal care. HEWs also mobilize pregnant women to seek care from skilled birth attendants—nurses,

---

Box 3.1 Ethiopia's Health Extension Program and Health Extension Workers

The Health Extension Program is an innovative, community-based program to deliver health services. The program's underlying assumption is that health can be enhanced in communities by raising awareness, diffusing knowledge through training, and creating model families, which exemplify sound health practices (completing immunization schedules, for example) and can share their knowledge and behavior.

The program has infrastructure and human staffing components. Every village with 5,000 residents is supposed to construct a health post and recruit two female health extension workers (HEWs) from the community. After one year of training in which they learn to implement 16 health extension packages, these women return to their community as frontline health care staff. The 16 packages are as follows:

- **Disease prevention and control** (3):
  - Human immunodeficiency virus (HIV)/acquired immune deficiency syndrome (AIDS) and other sexually transmitted infections; tuberculosis prevention and control
  - Malaria prevention and control
  - First aid emergency measures

---

box continues next page

Box 3.1 Ethiopia's Health Extension Program and Health Extension Workers *(continued)*

- **Family health** (5):
  - Maternal and child health
  - Family planning
  - Immunization
  - Nutrition
  - Adolescent reproductive health
- **Health education and communication**
- **Hygiene and environmental sanitation** (7):
  - Excreta disposal
  - Solid and liquid waste disposal
  - Water supply and safety measures
  - Food hygiene and safety measures
  - Healthy home environment
  - Control of insects and rodents
  - Personal hygiene.

The HEWs' main task is to increase awareness of disease prevention strategies. They may also supervise the intake of medication for tuberculosis and antiretroviral treatment for HIV/AIDS, conduct rapid diagnostic tests for malaria and administer malaria drugs, attend uncomplicated childbirths, and collect vital statistics; they are not allowed to administer antibiotics. A critical aspect of their work is to refer patients to nearby health centers as needed.

The Health Extension Program was piloted in five regions in 2002/03, with encouraging results. By mid-2008/09, the Federal Ministry of Health had successfully deployed over 30,190 HEWs throughout Ethiopia. Various evaluations have found the Health Extension Program to have very tangible effects on rural people's awareness of disease prevention, family health, hygiene, and environmental sanitation. The program now covers all of the country.

---

health officers, trained midwives, or physicians—whose positions are also funded from the local health budget, although they account for a smaller percentage of expenditure.

In other low-income countries, decentralized expenditure has been shown to improve health outcomes (Faguet and Ali 2009). Does this hold in Ethiopia? Woreda spending on health was analyzed with respect to four health-related outcomes: the Penta 3 vaccination rate; the percentage of pregnant women who receive antenatal care (ANC); the contraceptive acceptance rate (CAR); and the percentage of deliveries by skilled birth attendants (DelSBA). The first two outcomes are included in the results framework for the third phase of the PBS Program, while the latter two were included in the framework for the second phase. Each outcome is directly related to local spending on health. Control

Table 3.2 Association of Log of Per Capita Health Expenditure with Health Outcomes

	Indicator	Coefficient/(SE)	Significance
Log of expenditure	Log of Penta 3 vaccinations	−0.0578 (0.0276)	**
	Log of Penta 3 vaccinations on expenditure lagged one year	0.1116 (.0374)	***
	Log of antenatal care	0.0861 (0.0347)	**
	Log of contraceptive acceptance rate	−0.0064 (0.0410)	NS
	Log of contraceptive acceptance on expenditure lagged one year	0.1161 (.0491)	***
	Log of deliveries by skilled birth attendants	0.2669 (0.0747)	***

Source: Based on Poverty and Social Impact Analysis Database from 2008 to 2011.
Note: Number of observations is 1,664 for Penta 3, 2,277 for antenatal care, 2,243 for contraceptive acceptance rate, and 2,154 for deliveries by skilled birth attendants. Standard errors given in parentheses; *** indicates significance at 1 percent level, ** at 5 percent level.

variables included the per capita capital expenditure (at the regional level).[3] Table 3.2 presents the results of the log-linear regressions.

Increased health expenditures by woredas appear to improve the rates of Penta 3 vaccination, antenatal care, contraceptive use, and deliveries by skilled attendants. All of these results are significant, and all are robust to changes in specification. As with education, the model for health considers only per capita woreda-level spending on HEWs and health center staff; it does not consider nonsalary and capital costs, although clearly they can affect the results presented here. For example, HEWs can convince mothers to immunize their children, but the vaccines (financed separately from the health workers) must also be available.

The indicators included in the model directly reflect the responsibilities of HEWs, who account for most of the local recurrent health expenditure. HEWs mobilize the community during immunization campaigns. They are the frontline providers of antenatal care and the primary spokespersons in the community on the importance of contraception in family planning. Technically speaking, HEWs are not skilled birth attendants, but their referrals to those professionals influence the proportion of women who give birth with the assistance of a skilled attendant.

A smaller percentage of local health expenditure is directed to health centers. By federal mandate, each of the 3,000 health centers must be staffed by one to three health officers, depending on the characteristics of the host community. Each health officer is backed by a team of about four nurses and has at least one trained midwife. Each of the indicators assessed here can potentially be influenced by HEWs as well as health center staff, but except for deliveries by skilled birth attendants, most of the effects found in the analysis would be expected to arise from HEWs. Deliveries by skilled attendants would be influenced more equally by HEWs and health center staff.

A Positive Association between Woreda Block Grant Spending and Results in Agriculture

Ethiopia relies heavily on agriculture, which accounts for nearly half of gross domestic product (GDP) and employs around 80 percent of the population. The PBS Program supports agriculture by financing recurrent costs at the woreda level, mostly consisting of the costs of employing agricultural extension workers. Extension workers are trained to teach community members about the benefits of improved farming techniques, such as the appropriate use of improved seed and fertilizer, the importance of irrigation and erosion prevention, and other practices. About 20 percent of PBS funds go to the agricultural sector.

In agriculture, just as in health and education, expenditure levels increased rapidly between 2008 and 2011. Concomitant with this increase, the percentage of fields that use extension services has more than doubled. Figure 3.1 shows this trend for both variables. The agricultural data presented here and used in much of the analysis in the rest of this section are collected by the Central Statistical Agency as part of its annual Agriculture Sample Survey (AGSS). This survey obtains information from around 45,000 households and includes data from 500,000 fields in Ethiopia's nine regions as well as the city-state of Dire Dawa. The data are aggregated at the zonal level to be more representative of the underlying population.

Figure 3.1 Growth in Extension Services and Woredas' Expenditure on Agriculture, 2008–11

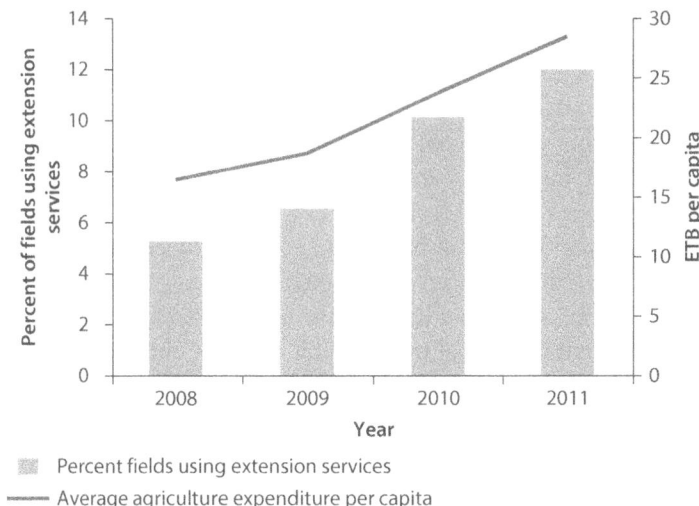

Percent fields using extension services

Average agriculture expenditure per capita

Source: World Bank, using AGSS data.
Note: ETB = Ethiopian birr.

Table 3.3 Effect on Farmers' Use of Extension Services of ETB 1 Per Capita Spending on Agricultural Extension Workers

Indicator	Coefficient/(SE)	Significance
Field using extension services	0.0008	**
	(0.0004)	
Field using improved seed	0.0002	*
	(0.0001)	
Field using fertilizer	0.0007	**
	(0.0003)	

Source: Based on probit models using cross-time pooled AGSS data from 2008 to 2011.
Note: AGSS data aggregated to the zonal level. Number of observations is 191. Controls include current and previous years' deviations from average rainfall (calculated as the average between 1996 and 2011), zonal poverty rate, percentage of the zone's population that is rural, and the ethnic groupings used in previous regressions. Standard errors are given in parentheses; ** indicates significance at 5 percent level, * at 10 percent level.

Zonal spending on agriculture significantly affects the use of a variety of improved farming techniques, as seen in the result of cross-time pooled regressions on AGSS data between 2008 and 2011 (table 3.3). The regressions for agriculture, like those for health and education, control for the percentage of the population that is rural and the ethnic composition of the zone. For each zone, deviation from the average rainfall (1996–2011) in the current and previous year is included as a predictor. In all regressions where an agricultural variable is included on the left-hand side, both the current year's as well as the previous year's deviation from average rainfall is a significant predictor.

Although the effects appear to be relatively small, several aspects of improved farming are significantly and positively associated with zonal per capita spending on agriculture. For every additional US$1 per capita spent, for example, the probability that a field in a given zone will benefit from extension services increases by about 0.2 percent (assuming an exchange rate of ETB 20 to US$1). Coefficients for the use of fertilizer and improved seed are smaller, but these practices remain positively and significantly associated with spending. In contrast, irrigation is not associated with higher spending. This result may be related to the higher capital costs associated with irrigating fields, and it would therefore depend more on zonal expenditure in the water sector than in agriculture.

Figure 3.2 shows the overall basket of crops produced by private farmers in 2011 by the amount produced (in quintals). Cereals (including barley, teff, wheat, sorghum, maize, oats, and rice) make up almost 75 percent of production. A further 15 percent consists of pulses (such as beans, chickpeas, and lentils) and root crops (such as potatoes, carrots, and onions). Enset, fruit crops, and coffee, which can be grown only in certain geographical areas, represent a smaller proportion of overall production.

Figure 3.2 Production by Crop, 2011

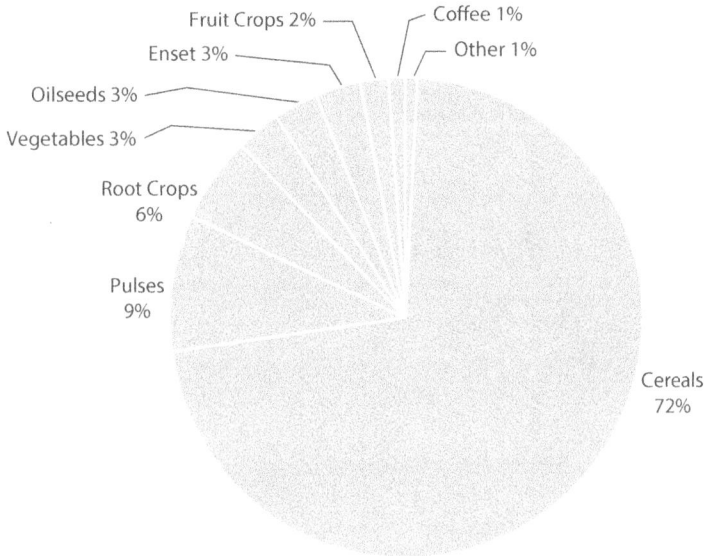

Source: World Bank estimates, AGSS, 2011.
Note: "Other" includes hops and chat. The figure does not include sugar, which is not often grown on private land.

The overall objective of spending on agriculture is to increase the productivity of farmers' fields (measured by yield, expressed here as the number of quintals produced per hectare of cultivated land). Cross-time pooled regressions between 2008 and 2011, with the log of yield of a specific category of crop (cereals, pulses, and so on) as the dependent variable, show strong positive relationships with log per capita recurrent agricultural spending and crop yields. Once again, control variables included each zone's percentage of rural population, overall poverty rate, the current and past years' deviation in rainfall from the average, and ethnic composition (this last variable helps to account for geographical heterogeneity in crop production).

Of the eight categories of crops grown in Ethiopia, five—cereals, vegetables, enset, fruit, and coffee, which represent about 85 percent of national agricultural production—show a positive and significant relationship with agricultural spending (table 3.4). These results, combined with the positive effect of spending on agricultural extension services, indicate that PBS Program funds play an important role in increasing farmers' productivity. As discussed, that role should be viewed as catalytic, because increased productivity also depends on other public and private spending, as well as investments in infrastructure, which are not reflected in this analysis.

Table 3.4 Association of Log of Per Capita Spending on Agricultural Extension Workers with Log of Yield

Independent variable	Dependent variable/indicator (yield in quintals/ha)	Coefficient/(SE)	Significance
Log of expenditure	Log of cereal yield	0.128 (0.0489)	***
	Log of pulse yield	−0.020 (0.0645)	NS
	Log of root crops yield	0.320 (0.2266)	NS
	Log of vegetable yield	0.582 (0.1330)	***
	Log of oilseed yield	−0.118 (0.1900)	NS
	Log of enset yield	2.397 (0.5766)	***
	Log of fruit yield	1.790 (0.2669)	***
	Log of coffee yield	1.267 (0.2342)	***

Source: Cross-time pooled AGSS data from 2008 to 2011.
Note: AGSS data aggregated to the zonal level. Number of observations: 167 (cereals), 159 (pulses), 152 (root crops), 167 (vegetables), 151 (oilseeds), 90 (enset), 162 (fruits), and 137 (coffee). Standard errors given in parentheses; *** indicates significance at 1 percent level; NS is not significant.

Notes

1. Secondary education expenditure is split between the woreda and the region, so it was not included in the analysis.

2. For example, improvements in the quality of education are supported under the General Education Quality Improvement Project, funded by the Government of Ethiopia, World Bank, DFID, United States Agency for International Development, and many others.

3. As noted in the discussion on methodology, other control variables included the rural/urban percentage and ethnicity.

CHAPTER 4

How Equitable Is Decentralized Spending at the Woreda Level?

The analyses in the previous sections find that decentralized spending on education, health, and agriculture at the woreda level is efficient, contributing positively and significantly to major development objectives in each sector. But has that spending also been equitable? This section examines several facets of the equity question, including the extent to which investments and outcomes may have varied by income group, gender, region, or ethnic group. The analysis should shed some empirical light on whether decentralized spending on service provision has furthered the government's objective of shared growth by targeting individuals in the two lowest wealth quintiles, and whether it has supported the constitutional objective of providing additional resources to historically underserved populations.

Woreda Block Grant Spending on Health Improves Outcomes, Especially for the Rural Poor

As mentioned, Ethiopia has met the Millennium Development Goals (MDG) of reducing the mortality rate by two-thirds in children under five years. This impressive achievement is due in no small part to rising local health budgets that pay for staff who provide the services and promote the behaviors that reduce under-five mortality. Similar improvements have been seen for other health indicators. Because Ethiopia conducted its Demographic and Health Survey (DHS) one year prior to the Promoting Basic Services (PBS) Program and then five years into its implementation, the data can reveal how the program may have affected individuals grouped by income level and location (in a rural or urban area). As most PBS resources flow to rural areas, this breakdown makes it possible to view the effects of health extension workers (HEWs) more clearly.

Figure 4.1 demonstrates the substantial improvement seen among rural people for all six health indicators between 2005 and 2011. It also shows that—in the majority of cases—the improvement was greatest among the bottom two wealth quintiles.[1] Contraceptive acceptance rates rose over 200 percent for the bottom two wealth quintiles, more than twice as much as in the top two

Figure 4.1 Percent Improvement in Selected Health Indicators Among Rural People Between 2005 and 2011, by Wealth Quintile

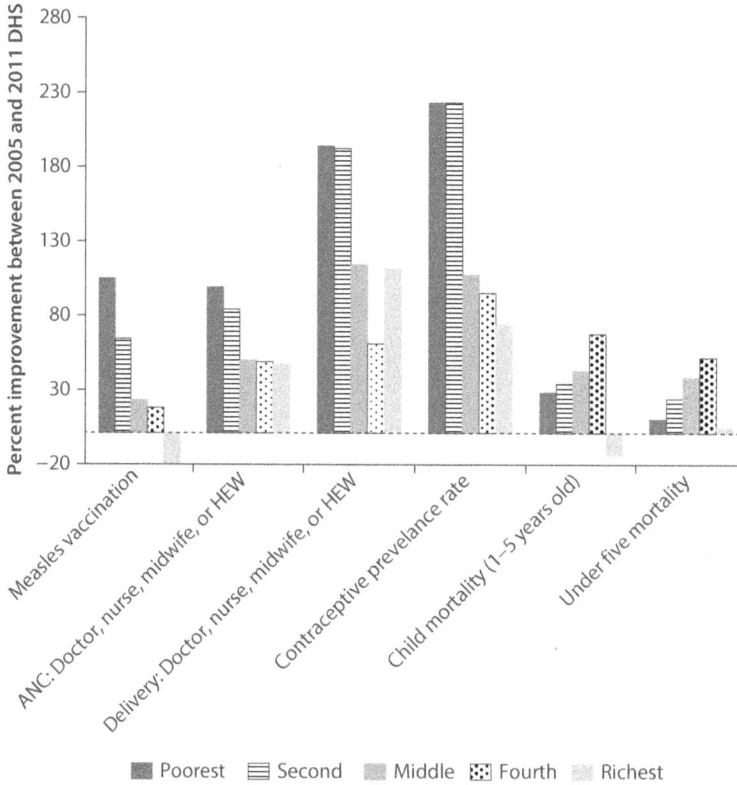

Source: World Bank, based on DHS 2005, 2011 data.
Note: ANC = Antenatal care; HEW = health extension worker.

quintiles. Similarly, for measles vaccination rates, antenatal care, and delivery by a skilled birth attendant, the poorest quintile showed the largest improvement. All of these outcomes are highly influenced by the presence of health workers in the field, which is financed by intergovernmental fiscal transfers (IGFTs) through the PBS Program.

The poorest quintiles also saw improvements in child and under-five mortality, more so than the richest quintile, but to a lesser degree than other quintiles. Outcomes for these indicators, unlike those for the other indicators, are particularly susceptible to factors outside the control of local recurrent health expenditure. Food security, nutritional status, and a mother's education all play a larger role than local health spending in driving these outcomes and can have an outsized effect among poorer individuals. It is telling that improvements in child mortality are larger than improvements in under-five mortality. The implication is that services—in the form of the health extension packages offered by HEWs (see box 3.1)—target children more than infants.

The probability of improvement in some of these outcomes can be estimated based on whether a household has had contact with an HEW (using 2011 DHS data on contacts with HEWs). For example, the 2011 survey asked whether a "family planning specialist or HEW" had visited the household in the past year. As many of the outcomes fit nicely into a binomial response (use of contraception versus no use of contraception, for instance), it is possible run a probit model in which the response to the question about an HEW visit is the right-hand-side variable and the left-hand side is either "success" or "failure" in achieving the health outcome. This approach assumes that an HEW can deliver multiple messages per contact, and not (for example) just a message about family planning. The model coefficients are then used to determine predicted probabilities for each specific outcome.

In fact, a household was more likely to achieve an outcome if an HEW had visited (table 4.1). This association holds across all outcomes for urban and rural locations, and for three of the four outcomes examined by wealth quintile, despite problems related to the small samples for some quintiles.[2] For example, pregnant women in the poorest rural households were 15 percent more likely to receive antenatal care and 12 percent more likely to vaccinate their child against measles if they had received a visit from an HEW than if they had not. The richer the household, the more likely it was to achieve many of the health outcomes examined here, probably because of unobserved factors, the foremost of which is probably women's education.

Table 4.1 Predicted Probabilities for "Successful" Health Outcomes by Place of Residence and Wealth Quintile if an HEW Visited the Household in the Past Year

Residence	Income quintile	Contraceptive use	Measles vaccination	ANC with doctor, nurse, midwife, or HEW	Delivery by doctor, nurse, midwife, or HEW
Urban	Total	0.071***	0.176***	0.124***	0.110***
Rural	Total	0.094***	0.144***	0.107***	0.017**
	Poorest	0.043**	0.115***	0.148***	NS
	Second	0.078***	0.106**	0.073***	NS
	Middle	0.069***	0.123***	0.097***	NS
	Fourth	0.108***	0.181***	0.096***	0.022*
	Richest	0.127**	0.189*	0.130**	NS

Source: Based on probit models.
Note: Number of observations varies by quintile, location, and outcome (see appendix A for details); *** indicates significance at 1% level, ** at 5 percent, and * at 10 percent. NS is not significant.

Incidence Analysis of Woreda Block Grant Spending on Health and Education

In examining the equity effects of the PBS Program, an important step was to analyze the incidence of health and education spending at the woreda level by wealth quintile. The most common form of incidence analysis relies on facility and service information by income group, but data constraints eliminated that approach. Instead, the analysis relied on DHS 2005 and 2011 data. The incidence of increase in per capita expenditures in the health and education sectors over 2005–11 was allocated by quintile based on the ratio of the improvement in results in that quintile to the average improvement in results (see appendix A, equation [A.4]). For education, one-result variable (net enrollment rate) was considered, whereas for health, the analysis used an average of the four results that can be affected by HEWs (vaccination, contraceptive use, antenatal care, and deliveries by skilled birth attendants). Given that the HEW system started between the two rounds of the DHS, the data constitute something of a natural experiment on the impact of HEWs. As noted, data on the use of HEWs' services from DHS 2011 indicate that HEWs have had a proportionately very strong effect on the four results just listed, particularly among individuals in the bottom quintiles.

For education, woreda-level spending appears to be pro-poor. The bottom 40 percent benefited from 56 percent of that expenditure, and the top quintile benefited from 13 percent. The incidence of per capita woreda-level spending on education was more than 2.5 times higher for the bottom quintile than for the top quintile (table 4.2). For health, a similar pattern emerged: 63 percent of the health expenditure at the woreda level accrued to the bottom 40 percent, whereas 10 percent accrued to the top quintile.[3] For someone in the bottom quintile, the benefit incidence of per capita woreda-level health spending was more than three times higher than it was for someone in the top quintile.

A forthcoming study of multiple countries,[4] using a standard methodology, corroborates the results obtained with the less-orthodox methodology used here. It also finds that woreda-level spending (financed through the PBS Program) is significantly more pro-poor than overall spending in education and health. Specifically, the overall incidence of all public education spending on the bottom 40 percent was 33 percent (it was 34 percent for health).

Table 4.2 Incidence of Woreda-Level Spending by Wealth Quintile

	Bottom 40% share (%)	Top 20% share (%)	Multiple by which bottom quintile exceeds top quintile
Education spending	56	13	2.7
Health spending	63	10	3.4
Combined education and health spending	58	12	2.9

Source: World Bank estimates based on several sources according to the methodology in appendix A of this book.

Catalytic Effect of Spending on Extension Services by Plot Size

Does the catalytic effect of spending on agricultural extension services vary by plot size? This question was explored using Agriculture Sample Survey (AGSS) data grouped by plot-size quintile. Regression analysis was done for each quintile to estimate the effect of each birr of spending on agricultural extension services on the probability that farmers in that quintile would use improved techniques (defined as improved seed, irrigation, or fertilizer).

Table 4.3 clearly shows that agricultural extension spending at the woreda level increases the use of improved farming techniques across all plot-size quintiles. The magnitude is relatively low in the bottom quintile, which may reflect financial constraints on purchasing inputs and otherwise investing in improved techniques. If so, this constraint could be addressed by improving access to rural finance.

Gender Equity Analysis for Woreda Block Grant Spending

Another major question related to equity is whether there is a gender bias in PBS expenditures on health, education, and agriculture. In health, the answer is an obvious yes. Women in the community, along with children, are the primary focus of outreach by HEWs and benefit from most of the packages they deliver (box 3.1). Spending on health by the woredas can also be considered pro-woman because so much of that spending is positively associated with increasing women's access to services that have a strong impact on reducing maternal mortality—including contraception, antenatal care, and assisted deliveries.

A more precise way to answer the gender equity question is to look at the association of expenditure with data on results disaggregated by gender, but such data are available only for education, and even then only for certain indicators. Table 4.4 provides key coefficients for education recurrent expenditure on net enrollment rate and net intake rate (NIR) at the primary level, disaggregated by

Table 4.3 Effect of ETB 1 Spending on Agricultural Extension Workers on Probability of Using Improved Farming Techniques, by Plot-Size Quintile, 2011

Plot-size quintile	Any improved technique
Smallest and poorest	0.000322***
Second smallest	0.000344***
Middle	0.000524***
Fourth	0.000667***
Largest and richest	0.000818***

Source: Based on probit models using AGSS data.
Note: Cross-sectional data with 303,242 observations (which are plots, not total household land holdings). Standard errors given in parentheses; *** indicates significance at the 1 percent level. NS is not significant.

Table 4.4 Association of Log of Education Expenditure with Log of Net Enrollment Rate and Log of Net Intake Rate, by Gender

Independent variable	Dependent variable/ indicator	Coefficient/(SE)	Significance
Log of expenditure	Log of NER grades 1–8, male	0.115 (0.0116)	***
	Log of NER grades 1–8, female	0.158 (0.0137)	***
	Log of NIR grades 1–8, male	0.390 (0.0240)	***
	Log of NIR grades 1–8, female	0.430 (0.0269)	***

Source: Based on Poverty and Social Impact Analysis Database from 2008 to 2011.
Note: Number of observations is 2,583 for NER and 2,464 for NIR; *** indicates significance at 1 percent level. NS is not significant. NER = net enrollment rate; NIR = net intake rate.

gender. The coefficient for female primary school students is slightly higher than for males for both the net enrollment and intake rates, but this difference is not significant. The important finding here is that there is no negative bias against females in expenditure on education, the sector that receives the bulk of PBS Program funds.

By contrast, evidence from the agricultural sector implies an apparent bias in outcomes (female farmers are less likely to benefit from extension services), which was also found in a study by the International Food Policy Research Institute (Ragasa et al. 2012). The reasons for this bias are not clear, but it could reflect a wide range of circumstances, such as a tendency for extension workers to target male farmers (87 percent of Ethiopia's farmer are male), a tendency of women farmers to grow crops of different types or quality than those grown by men, or a tendency of female farmers to have smaller holdings.

Table 4.5 shows the probability that improved farming techniques will be used on a field, disaggregated by the gender of the head of the household. About 13 percent of fields in the sample are farmed by female-headed households; such fields are significantly less likely to benefit from extension services, though the effect is relatively small. Again, in interpreting these results, it is important to bear in mind that many other factors also influence the adoption of improved farming techniques, the sample size for female-headed households is small, and the quality of the data could be improved. Further analysis is required to determine whether extension workers are indeed preferentially targeting fields owned by men and to develop policy responses based on the evidence.

Table 4.5 Predicted Probabilities of Improved Farming Techniques Being Used on a Field, by Gender of Household Head, 2011

Household head	Probability that an improved technique is used on a field
Male	0.000027***
Female	−0.000023***

Source: Based on probit models using AGSS data.
Note: Number of observations is 303,242. Standard errors given in parenthesis; *** indicates significance at 1 percent level.

Notes

1. Owing to the small urban population in Ethiopia, the samples for the wealth quintiles contained too few observations to be representative.

2. For example, only 1,000 deliveries attended by a doctor, nurse, midwife, or HEW were reported, making it difficult to obtain reliable estimates when the data were disaggregated by wealth quintile.

3. Thirty-five percent of woreda health and education expenditures accrued to the bottom quintile.

4. See Woldehanna, Tsehaye, and Hill (forthcoming).

CHAPTER 5

The Federal System's Role in Helping Lagging Areas and Groups

The Government of Ethiopia has made the development of historically disadvantaged groups and areas a priority. Its system of fiscal decentralization transfers funds to local governments based on formulas applied at the federal and regional levels, and level of development is a primary element of those formulas. The following sections examine the allocation of subnational expenditures by geographical area and ethnic group.

Regionally Disaggregated Analysis of Woreda Block Grant Spending

Figure 5.1 is a simple scatterplot of per capita subnational expenditures across Ethiopia's 718 woredas in 2010, in which each woreda is represented by a dot. Identification numbers assigned by region are on the x-axis, which naturally groups woredas by region, demarcated in red. The dashed yellow line shows the average expenditure in Ethiopia across all woreda, at Ethiopian birr (ETB) 183 per capita.

Most woredas fall into a spending band of ETB 150–250 per capita. The lower outliers cluster near this band, whereas some outliers range as high as ETB 1,000 per capita. Taking ETB 385 per capita, 110 percent above the national average, as the cut-off. Table 5.1 provides data on the higher outliers.

Seven of the woredas that spend the most on basic services, including the five highest observations nationwide, are in Gambella. More than 50 percent of the woredas in Gambella spend more than 110 percent of the national average on the basic service sectors, and so do six woredas in Beneshangul-Gemuz, representing 30 percent of the woredas in that region. Gambella and Beneshangul-Gemuz are among the regions that historically have been the most economically deprived. Another six woredas where per capita spending on basic services is higher than the average are in Tigray. Among the much larger regions that have dominated government and the economy since the days of the empire, Amhara has only two woredas where spending exceeds ETB 385 per capita, and Oromia

Figure 5.1 Woreda Total Recurrent Expenditure Per Capita, 2010

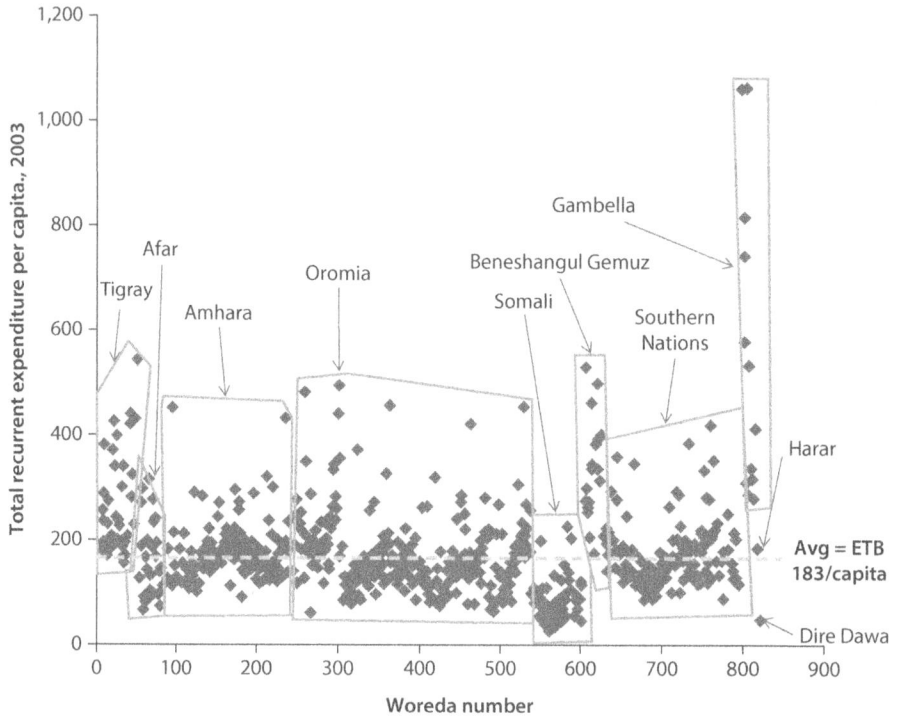

Source: World Bank estimates based on data described in appendix A of this book.

Table 5.1 Woredas Spending More Than 110 Percent of the National Average on Basic Services, by Region, 2010

Region	No. woredas	No. woredas above 110% national average	Percent of woredas above 70% national average (%)
Tigray	46	6	13
Afar	30	0	0
Amhara	137	2	2
Oromia	278	6	2
Somali	48	0	0
Beneshangul-Gemuz	20	6	30
SNNP	144	2	1
Gambella	13	7	54
Harari	1	0	0
Dire Dawa	1	0	0

Source: World Bank.
Note: SNNP = Southern Nations, Nationalities, and Peoples (Region).

has six. The observations for the lowest spending levels appear in Amhara, Oromia, and Somali. In terms of expenditure per capita, then, the current system broadly favors Ethiopia's historically disadvantaged regions at the expense of the historically dominant ones. At the same time, table 5.1 shows that the federal system also prioritizes underserved areas in regions with the larger, more established ethnic groups, such as the Amhara, Oromo, and Tigrayan. The next section looks in greater detail at Woreda Block Grant spending by ethnic group.

Ethnically Disaggregated Analysis of Woreda Block Grant Spending

Ethiopia's complex history explains some of the regional differences in development.[1] In the late nineteenth century, areas consisting of today's Beneshangul-Gemuz, Gambella, Southern Nations and Nationalities, Afar, Oromia, and Somali Regions were brought under the feudal system of the Ethiopian Empire, based in the highlands of north-central Ethiopia. Relations between the newly integrated areas and the historic center of the empire were troubled. Owing to the structural weakness of the center, successive Ethiopian governments did not command effective control over the periphery. Similarly, exploitive economic policies promulgated by the center resulted in visible marginalization and relative underdevelopment at the periphery of the empire. This dynamic persisted through the socialist era. It was not until 1991, when the Ethiopian People's Revolutionary Democratic Front came into power, that ethnic federalism took root in Ethiopia.

A primary objective of this new government was to reverse the policy of ethnic homogenization and promote "equitable and broadly shared" economic growth among all regions. Achieving this objective involved affirmative action in the form of increased budget allocations to historically less developed regions. Preferential treatment of previously disadvantaged ethnic groups within Ethiopia is helping to create a more equitable base for development. The small lagging groups appear to be faring well, yet at the woreda level, the largest lagging group—the Somali—is not receiving the additional resources per capita warranted by its development status. The reason for this disparity appears to be that during the four years covered in this analysis, the Somali Region transferred only 49 percent of its Federal Block Grant resources to woredas, compared to the average of 73 percent for all other regions.[2]

Ethiopia has 91 registered linguistic groups and 93 registered ethnicities, making it impractical to include a full set of dummies for either of those variables, let alone both, in the econometric estimations. Most of these language and ethnic groups account for less than 1 percent of the population. Given that the five largest ethnicities are heavily concentrated in their five home regions, controlling for region in the regression models is substantially similar to controlling for ethnicity. For that reason, the econometric models focus on smaller ethnic groups, particularly a subset of historically disadvantaged groups.

Using demographic data from the 2007 census, the analysis focuses on the Nuwer and Anyiwak[3] from Gambella. All other ethnicities, representing less than 1.5 percent of the population, are combined into a separate group ("other small").

Total recurrent expenditure per capita at the woreda level between 2008 and 2011 is then compared for these categories versus the largest ethnic groupings in the country, omitted from the estimations, such as Amhara, Oromo, and Tigrayan. Other estimations not reported here substituted linguistic dummies for ethnic dummies, with no significant change in the results. Dummies for Ethiopia's 12 regions also mirror the main findings with respect to large versus small ethnic/ linguistic groups, and they did not substantially change any of the other findings.

Table 5.2 provides the key results. It shows that ethnicities with a smaller proportion of the population receive a larger share of recurrent expenditure, particularly the Anyiwak from Gambella, with ETB 770 more per capita than larger groups. The Nuwer receive substantially more per capita as well—ETB 142. As the positive significant coefficient for the "other small" category shows, ethnic groups in that category, which are more likely to be at a relative historical disadvantage in development, receive a significantly higher proportion of recurrent expenditure.

Table 5.2 Selected Ethnicities' Influence on Total Woreda Recurrent Expenditure Per Capita

Indicator: Ethnic percentage	Coefficient/(SE)	Significance
Nuwer	141.5	***
	(36.92)	
Anyiwak	769.5	***
	(43.82)	
Gemuz	280.3	***
	(39.03)	
Konso	−10.5	NS
	(71.85)	
Somali[a]	−66.5	***
	(14.26)	
Afar	−0.5	NS
	(17.56)	
Other small	32.9	**
	(12.94)	
Historically developed groups (Oromo, Amhara, Gurage, Tigray)	24.9	**
	(10.79)	

Source: Based on Poverty and Social Impact Analysis Database from 2008 to 2011.
Note: "Other small" includes: Agew Awi, Agew Hamyra, Alaba, Argoba, Ari, Arborie, Bacha, Basketo, Bench, Berta, Bodi, Brayle, Burji, Bena, Chara, Dasenech, Dawuro, Debase Gewada, Derashe, Dime, Dizi, Donga, Fedashe, Gamo, Gebato, Gedeo, Gedicho, Gidole, Goffa, Guagu, Hareri, Hamer, Irob, Kefficho, Kembata, Konta, Komo, Koro, Koyego, Kunama, Karo, Kusumie, Malie, Mao, Mareko, Mashola, Mere, Meenite, Messengo, Mejenger, Mossiye, Mursi, Murle, Nao, Nyanegatome, Oida, Qebena, Qechem, Qewama, Shekecho, Sheko, Shinasha, Silte, Surma, She, Timebaro, Tsemay, Upo, Werji, Yem, Zeyese, and Zelmam; *** indicates significance at the 1% level, ** at 5%. NS is not significant.
a. Data for Somali woredas may be understated, as some expenditures normally paid by woredas in other regions are paid regionally due to security and capacity constraints.

A central question posed in this study is whether woredas with a high proportion of historically disadvantaged ethnic groups are favored or disfavored by fiscal transfers. The higher distributions to such groups reported here indicate that PBS Program funding in fact targets their development needs.

Notes

1. For more details see appendix C.

2. The average excludes Addis Ababa, a large city where woredas need to do less with regard to basic service provision and other development targets. Note that data on spending at the woreda level may be understated in Somali Region; some expenditures normally paid by woredas in other regions are paid regionally due to security and capacity constraints.

3. Nuwer is also spelled as Nuer. Note as well that the census spelling for Anyiwak is used here; alternative forms include Anuak and Anyiwa, among others.

Conclusions and Recommendations

The evidence assembled here implies that decentralized spending at the woreda level is both effective and pro-poor. The estimates imply that the returns to this spending are far from decreasing, which means that Ethiopia has scope to increase spending and speed its achievement of the Millennium Development Goals (MDGs). In agriculture, the impact of decentralized spending could be improved by providing better access to rural finance for the poorest producers.

Some caveats are needed with respect to these findings. In education, spending on materials and other quality drivers is not included in Woreda Block Grants. Teachers' salaries, which are included, usually constitute 80–90 percent of education spending. In health, spending in the woredas does not drive the results but should be regarded more as a catalyst to increase the effectiveness of systemwide spending. The agricultural extension workers supported through the Woreda Block Grants play a similarly catalytic role.

Some historically disadvantaged areas are significantly favored under the current spending framework. Expenditure is broadly equal across Ethiopia's woredas, with the striking exception of a small number of woredas concentrated in the country's most disadvantaged regions, which receive significantly greater resources. Woredas receiving the least resources are concentrated in the more developed, historically dominant regions. Four majority-Anyiwak woredas are noteworthy for receiving more public resources than all other woredas in the nation. At the very least, the additional resources appear to help disadvantaged groups catch up.

The lack of data from the period prior to decentralization prevents an analysis of the effects of decentralization *per se* on financial flows, sectoral outputs, or substantive outputs. Even so, data gathered at the woreda level as decentralization unfolds can contribute to the debate about the effectiveness of woreda-controlled service provision. Based on the data available to date, this study finds that contrary to the predictions of some public management theories, the decentralized provision of services in Ethiopia is not increasing regional, ethnic, or gender inequalities in investment inputs or service outputs. Indeed, the opposite seems to be true for education and health, where the impact of Promoting Basic

Services (PBS)-financed intergovernmental fiscal transfer (IGFT) resources was disproportionately high among the bottom two quintiles and women. In sum, support for decentralized services in Ethiopia appears to be an effective use of development partners' resources from both an efficiency and equity perspective.

The only exception to these findings is agriculture, for which the impact of PBS-financed IGFT expenditure was smaller for the bottom quintile. In this instance, a wide array of factors is likely to be at work, especially poor farmers' inability to buy inputs or the poor quality of their land.

Although quantitative evidence is unavailable at present, descriptive evidence from the first phase of the Ethiopia Social Accountability Program implies that structured feedback sessions involving citizens and service providers are strengthening citizens' participation in pilot areas. That evidence, together with the strong guidance emerging from governance and accountability theory, would appear to favor the continued application of social accountability tools and the development of policies to sustain their use in the Ethiopian context. This conclusion will be verified when the impact assessment for the second phase of the Ethiopia Social Accountability Program becomes available (the only data available now are from the baseline survey).

A final important point is that the difficulty of conducting subnational empirical work on Ethiopia cannot be overstated. Creating the database for this study required considerable effort and improvisation on the part of the research team. The resulting standardized database of woreda-level expenditures and characteristics, which will be made public, is a major output of this study. The data will be augmented with new data collected under the third phase of the PBS Program and used in future research related to the program. It is hoped that in time this dataset will become a useful tool for researchers and students elsewhere in Africa and beyond.

Detailed Methodology and Data Sources

Methodology

This study relies on a database of woreda-level recurrent expenditure and outcome information for a variety of health and education indicators between 2008 and 2011. The data are complemented by information from the 2007 census on the demographic characteristics of each woreda, including population, shares of population by ethnic group and by rural or urban residence, and other variables. Econometric modeling is used to assess the impact of increased local spending on the expansion of basic services and outcomes, and by extension the efficiency of the PBS Program in meeting its development objective.

Cross-time pooled regressions with the outcome variable of interest on the left-hand side were run to evaluate the impact of per capita sector expenditure, controlling for rural/urban percentage and ethnicity, over the four years. The outcome indicators evaluated are mostly drawn from the Promoting Basic Services (PBS) Results Framework. No reliable outcome data at the local level could be gathered for agriculture, water supply, or roads, however, so alternative approaches were used (zonal data on outcomes for agriculture, and desk reviews for water supply and roads). Note that expenditure on water supply and roads accounts for 3 percent of woreda-level spending; agriculture, education, and health, which are fully analyzed, account for the remaining 97 percent. National surveys (DHS [Demographic and Health Survey] and Agriculture Sample Survey [AGSS]) complement the analysis from the woreda-level database.

The analysis proceeded in three stages. Stage I follows the approach of Faguet (2012) and Faguet and Sánchez (2013), examining the relationship between woreda-level spending (a proxy for service delivery, as discussed in the main text) in each sector on results in those sectors. That is,

$$\ln O_{mt} = \alpha + \zeta \ln E_{mt} + \beta R_m + \delta \mathbf{C}_m + \eta \ln K_{mt} + \tau_t + \varepsilon_{mt} \qquad (A.1)$$

where $\ln O$ is different outcome variables, such as the net enrollment rate or use of antenatal care, capturing key outcomes in each sector; E is yearly expenditure per capita in the relevant sector; K is capital expenditure per capita; R is the percentage of rural population in each woreda; τ is a variable for the year to control for the time-series effect in this cross-time pooled dataset; and $\mathbf{C}$ is a vector of demographic controls, capturing the percentage of certain historically disadvantaged ethnic groups that are the focus of the analysis—all indexed by woreda m and, for expenditure, by year t. R and $\mathbf{C}$ are taken from the census and do not change over time. The above was also estimated using the quadratic form to check for decreasing marginal returns.

$$O_{mt} = \alpha + \zeta E_{mt} + \lambda E_{mt}{}^2 + \beta R_m + \delta \mathbf{C}_m + \eta K_{mt} + \tau_t + \varepsilon_{mt} \tag{A.2}$$

As Yang (2012, 1) indicates:

> Interpreting the results of an analysis with log transformed data may be challenging.... A log transformation is often useful for data which exhibit right skewness (positively skewed), and for data where the variability of residuals increases for larger values of the dependent variable. When a variable is log transformed, note that simply taking the anti-log of your parameters will not properly back transform into the original metric used. To properly back transform into the original scale we need to understand some details about the log-normal distribution. In probability theory, a log-normal distribution is a continuous probability distribution of a random variable whose logarithm is normally distributed.

Finally, a linear version was also tested.

$$O_{mt} = \alpha + \zeta E_{mt} + \beta R_m + \delta \mathbf{C}_m + \eta K_{mt} + \tau_t + \varepsilon_{mt} \tag{A.3}$$

For all three equations, it is expected $\delta O/\delta E \geq 0$ and $\delta O/\delta K \geq 0$. Similarly, $\delta \ln O/\delta \ln E \geq 0$ (the first partial derivative), while in equation (A.2) $\delta^2 O/\delta^2 E \leq 0$ (the second partial derivative). The expected results imply a positive association of the dependent variable with the independent variable (per capita woreda expenditures in the sector). Equation (A.2) also tests whether the association is positive with a declining marginal impact.

The form estimated in equation (A.2) allows us to verify if the returns to scale are declining. The form in equation (A.1) reduces the effect of extreme values on the results.

Stage II conducts an incidence analysis of woreda-level spending by quintile, using the wealth quintile breakdown from the DHS survey. The incidence analysis was done by allocating improvements in health and education outcomes to each quintile by pro-rating the expenditure increases to each quintile by the improvement in outcomes achieved for that quintile, controlling for the average improvement for all groups. That is,

$$\Delta E_i = (\Delta I_i / \Delta I) * \Delta E \tag{A.4}$$

where ΔE_i is the per capita increase in expenditure for quintile i, ΔE is the overall increase in expenditure per capita, ΔI_i is the change in outcome change for quintile i, and ΔI the outcome change for all quintiles. The results indicator for education was the net enrollment rate, which is directly affected by teachers recruited locally by the woreda. For health, the results indicator is an average of four indicators that are directly affected by locally recruited HEWs: increased use of contraception, increased rates of immunization, increased use of antenatal care, and increased use of skilled birth attendants.

Stage III examines the link between woreda expenditure and sectoral results for different wealth quintiles, using DHS household survey data and limited dependent variable estimations as follows:

$$P_{i,j} = f(\Theta, \alpha) \qquad\qquad\qquad (A.5)$$

In equation (A.5), $P_{i,j}$ is the probability of improvement for household j in quintile i, and α indicates whether the household has had contact with a health worker. Θ is a "yes" or "no" variable, with "yes" being coded 1 and "no" coded 0.

This three-stage analysis was limited to sectors with reliable data on woreda-level results and corresponding household survey data on health and education. In the case of education, the third-stage test was not considered necessary due the direct linkage between woreda-level spending, which is mostly for teachers, and the net enrollment rate. It was needed for health, however, because the linkage is less direct. Woreda-level spending is on HEWs; therefore, the link between contact with health extension workers (HEWs) and health sector outcomes was tested using DHS data. As discussed in the main text, data limitations prevented incidence analysis for agriculture, but the effect of agricultural extension services was analyzed by plot-size quintile. No in-depth analysis was possible for water supply or roads.

The Poverty and Social Impact Analysis Database

The database constructed for this study includes data from five ministries—Health, Education, Agriculture, Water and Energy, and Finance and Economic Development—as well as the Central Statistical Agency and the Disaster Risk Management and Food Security Sector of the Ministry of Agriculture. It also includes woreda-level poverty rates calculated by the Central Statistical Agency with World Bank technical assistance. As standardization of woreda codes and the transliteration of Amharic names into Latin script is not yet consistent across ministries, much time was dedicated to presenting information on woredas from various sources in one consistent format, based on the Population and Housing Census of Ethiopia (2007) codes.

The woreda database includes information on expenditures by sector and year; key results for health and education; and information on ethnicity, the frequency of droughts, and other control variables. In addition, regional data on per capita capital expenditures and zonal data on crop yields have been linked to the woreda data. The plan is to update the database yearly, incorporating new results for each sector as they become available, and adding other useful data, such as local-level capital expenditure through time. The database has already been revised to incorporate education data broken down into grades 1–4 and 5–8, which were not available for the analysis presented here. Other researchers are invited to supplement the database with data collected as part of their own research programs. The analysis of these data is a public good, and they should be publicly available for researchers in Africa and elsewhere. Table A.1 lists variables in the database along with the corresponding administrative levels and years.

Table A.1 Variables in the Poverty and Social Impact Analysis Database, by Administrative Level

Sector	Variable	Administrative level	Years
Demographic	Population: Total	Woreda, zone, region	2007
	Population: Urban	Woreda, zone, region	2007
	Population: Rural	Woreda, zone, region	2007
	Religion[a]	Woreda	2007
	Mother tongue[b]	Woreda	2007
	Ethnicity[c]	Woreda	2007
Expenditure	Approved recurrent budget: Agriculture, Education, Health, Water	Woreda	2008, 2009, 2010, 2011
	Adjusted recurrent budget: Agriculture, Education, Health, Water	Woreda	2008, 2009, 2010, 2011
	Annual recurrent expenditure: Agriculture, Education, Health, Water	Woreda	2008, 2009, 2010, 2011
	Over/under recurrent expenditure: Agriculture, Education, Health, Water	Woreda	2008, 2009, 2010, 2011
	Capital expenditure	Region	2008, 2009, 2010, 2011
Meteorological	Number of years of drought between 1974 and 2007	Woreda	NA
	Deviation from average rainfall between 1986 and 2011	Zone	2008, 2009, 2010, 2011
	Average rainfall between 1986 and 2011	Zone	2008, 2009, 2010, 2011
Poverty	Poverty rate	Woreda, zone	2011
	Standard error of poverty rate	Woreda	2011
	Gini coefficient	Woreda, zone	2011
	Depth of poverty	Woreda, zone	2011
	Significantly poorer than average	Woreda	2011
Water and sanitation	Safe water access	Woreda, zone	2011
	Latrine access	Woreda, zone	2011
	Safe water usage	Woreda, zone	2011
	Safe water access at health facilities	Woreda, zone	2011
	Safe water access at schools	Woreda, zone	2011
	Any latrines at schools	Woreda, zone	2011
	Improved latrines at schools	Woreda, zone	2011

table continues next page

Table A.1 Variables in the Poverty and Social Impact Analysis Database, by Administrative Level *(continued)*

Sector	Variable	Administrative level	Years
Education	Gross enrollment rate: Grades 1–8, total	Woreda, zone, region	2007, 2008, 2009, 2010, 2011
	Gross enrollment rate: Grades 1–8, male	Woreda, zone, region	2007, 2008, 2009, 2010, 2011
	Gross enrollment rate: Grades 1–8, female	Woreda, zone, region	2007, 2008, 2009, 2010, 2011
	Gross enrollment rate: Grades 1–4, total	Woreda, zone, region	2007, 2008, 2009, 2010, 2011
	Gross enrollment rate: Grades 1–4, male	Woreda, zone, region	2007, 2008, 2009, 2010, 2011
	Gross enrollment rate: Grades 1–4, female	Woreda, zone, region	2007, 2008, 2009, 2010, 2011
	Gross enrollment rate: Grades 5–8, total	Woreda, zone, region	2007, 2008, 2009, 2010, 2011
	Gross enrollment rate: Grades 5–8, male	Woreda, zone, region	2007, 2008, 2009, 2010, 2011
	Gross enrollment rate: Grades 5–8, female	Woreda, zone, region	2007, 2008, 2009, 2010, 2011
	Net enrollment rate: Grades 1–8, total	Woreda, zone, region	2007, 2008, 2009, 2010, 2011
	Net enrollment rate: Grades 1–8, male	Woreda, zone, region	2007, 2008, 2009, 2010, 2011
	Net enrollment rate: Grades 1–8, female	Woreda, zone, region	2007, 2008, 2009, 2010, 2011
	Net enrollment rate: Grades 1–4, total	Woreda, zone, region	2007, 2008, 2009, 2010, 2011
	Net enrollment rate: Grades 1–4, male	Woreda, zone, region	2007, 2008, 2009, 2010, 2011
	Net enrollment rate: Grades 1–4, female	Woreda, zone, region	2007, 2008, 2009, 2010, 2011
	Net enrollment rate: Grades 5–8, total	Woreda, zone, region	2007, 2008, 2009, 2010, 2011
	Net enrollment rate: Grades 5–8, male	Woreda, zone, region	2007, 2008, 2009, 2010, 2011
	Net enrollment rate: Grades 5–8, female	Woreda, zone, region	2007, 2008, 2009, 2010, 2011
	Net intake rate: Grades 1–8, total	Woreda	2007, 2008, 2009, 2010, 2011
	Net intake rate: Grades 1–8, male	Woreda	2007, 2008, 2009, 2010, 2011
	Net intake rate: Grades 1–8, female	Woreda	2007, 2008, 2009, 2010, 2011
	Apparent intake rate: Grades 1–8, total	Woreda	2007, 2008, 2009, 2010, 2011

table continues next page

Improving Basic Services for the Bottom Forty Percent • http://dx.doi.org/10.1596/978-1-4648-0331-4

Table A.1 Variables in the Poverty and Social Impact Analysis Database, by Administrative Level *(continued)*

Sector	Variable	Administrative level	Years
	Apparent intake rate: Grades 1–8, male	Woreda	2007, 2008, 2009, 2010, 2011
	Apparent intake rate: Grades 1–8, female	Woreda	2007, 2008, 2009, 2010, 2011
	Primary schools	Woreda	2008, 2009, 2010, 2011
	Pupil-teacher ratio	Woreda	2007, 2008, 2009, 2010, 2011
	Section-student ratio	Woreda	2008, 2009, 2010, 2011
	Dropout rate: Grade 1, total	Woreda	2007, 2008, 2009, 2010
	Dropout rate: Grade 1, male	Woreda	2007, 2008, 2009, 2010
	Dropout rate: Grade 1, female	Woreda	2007, 2008, 2009, 2010
	Dropout rate: Grade 2, total	Woreda	2007, 2008, 2009, 2010
	Dropout rate: Grade 2, male	Woreda	2007, 2008, 2009, 2010
	Dropout rate: Grade 2, female	Woreda	2007, 2008, 2009, 2010
	Dropout rate: Grade 3, total	Woreda	2007, 2008, 2009, 2010
	Dropout rate: Grade 3, male	Woreda	2007, 2008, 2009, 2010
	Dropout rate: Grade 3, female	Woreda	2007, 2008, 2009, 2010
	Dropout rate: Grade 4, total	Woreda	2007, 2008, 2009, 2010
	Dropout rate: Grade 4, male	Woreda	2007, 2008, 2009, 2010
	Dropout rate: Grade 4, female	Woreda	2007, 2008, 2009, 2010
	Dropout rate: Grade 5, total	Woreda	2007, 2008, 2009, 2010
	Dropout rate: Grade 5, male	Woreda	2007, 2008, 2009, 2010
	Dropout rate: Grade 5, female	Woreda	2007, 2008, 2009, 2010
	Dropout rate: Grade 6, total	Woreda	2007, 2008, 2009, 2010
	Dropout rate: Grade 6, male	Woreda	2007, 2008, 2009, 2010
	Dropout rate: Grade 6, female	Woreda	2007, 2008, 2009, 2010

table continues next page

Table A.1 Variables in the Poverty and Social Impact Analysis Database, by Administrative Level *(continued)*

Sector	Variable	Administrative level	Years
	Dropout rate: Grade 7, total	Woreda	2007, 2008, 2009, 2010
	Dropout rate: Grade 7, male	Woreda	2007, 2008, 2009, 2010
	Dropout rate: Grade 7, female	Woreda	2007, 2008, 2009, 2010
	Repetition rate: Grades 1–8, total	Woreda, zone, region	2007, 2008, 2009, 2010
	Repetition rate: Grades 1–8, male	Woreda, zone, region	2007, 2008, 2009, 2010
	Repetition rate: Grades 1–8, female	Woreda, zone, region	2007, 2008, 2009, 2010
Health	Number of health posts	Woreda	2011
	Number of health centers	Woreda	2011
	Contraceptive acceptance rate	Woreda	2008, 2010, 2011
	Antenatal care	Woreda	2008, 2010, 2011
	Deliveries by skilled birth attendants	Woreda	2008, 2010, 2011
	Prevention of mother-to-child transmission tested	Woreda	2008, 2010, 2011
	Penta3 vaccination rate	Woreda	2008, 2010, 2011
	Measles vaccination rate	Woreda	2008, 2010, 2011
	Fully immunized rate	Woreda	2008, 2010, 2011
	Tuberculosis detection rate	Woreda	2008, 2010, 2011
	Tuberculosis treatment rate	Woreda	2010, 2011
	Tuberculosis cure rate	Woreda	2010, 2011
Agriculture	Total cultivatable area (hectares)	Zone	2008, 2009, 2010, 2011
	Total production (quintals)	Zone	2008, 2009, 2010, 2011
	Number of fields	Zone	2008, 2009, 2010, 2011
	Source of irrigation[d]	Zone	2008, 2009, 2010, 2011
	Number of fields irrigated	Zone	2008, 2009, 2010, 2011
	Number of fields using extension services	Zone	2008, 2009, 2010, 2011
	Number of fields using fertilizer	Zone	2008, 2009, 2010, 2011
	Number of fields using improved seed	Zone	2008, 2009, 2010, 2011
	Cereals: Area cultivated (hectares)[e]	Zone	2008, 2009, 2010, 2011
	Cereals: Production (quintals)	Zone	2008, 2009, 2010, 2011
	Pulses: Area cultivated (hectares)	Zone	2008, 2009, 2010, 2011

table continues next page

Table A.1 Variables in the Poverty and Social Impact Analysis Database, by Administrative Level *(continued)*

Sector	Variable	Administrative level	Years
	Pulses: Production (quintals)	Zone	2008, 2009, 2010, 2011
	Oilseeds: Area cultivated (hectares)	Zone	2008, 2009, 2010, 2011
	Oilseeds: Production (quintals)	Zone	2008, 2009, 2010, 2011
	Vegetables: Area cultivated (hectares)	Zone	2008, 2009, 2010, 2011
	Vegetables: Production (quintals)	Zone	2008, 2009, 2010, 2011
	Root crops: Area cultivated (hectares)	Zone	2008, 2009, 2010, 2011
	Root crops: Production (quintals)	Zone	2008, 2009, 2010, 2011
	Fruit: Area cultivated (hectares)	Zone	2008, 2009, 2010, 2011
	Fruit: Production (quintals)	Zone	2008, 2009, 2010, 2011
	Coffee: Area cultivated (hectares)	Zone	2008, 2009, 2010, 2011
	Coffee: Production (quintals)	Zone	2008, 2009, 2010, 2011
	Chat: Area cultivated (hectares)	Zone	2008, 2009, 2010, 2011
	Chat: Production (quintals)	Zone	2008, 2009, 2010, 2011
	Enset: Area cultivated (hectares)	Zone	2008, 2009, 2010, 2011
	Enset: Production (quintals)	Zone	2008, 2009, 2010, 2011

Source: World Bank. Data sources for variables include: Annual Agriculture Sample Surveys, Central Statistical Agency, 2008–11; Education Management Information System Administrative Data, Ministry of Education, 2007–11; Ethiopia Demographic and Health Surveys, 2005 and 2011; Health Management Information System administrative data, Ministry of Health, 2007–11; Poverty Map with woreda and zonal poverty rates, Central Statistical Agency, 2012; Population and Housing Census of Ethiopia (using 10 percent sample), Central Statistical Agency, 2007; Water, Sanitation, and Hygiene (WASH) Census, Ministry of Water and Energy, 2012; Woreda Annual Progress Reports, Ministry of Health, 2007–11; and woreda-level recurrent expenditures in basic services, Ministry of Finance and Economic Development, 2007–11.
a. Orthodox, Protestant, Catholic, Muslim, Traditionalist, and other.
b. Afarigna, Agew Awinigigna, Agew Kamyrigna, Alabigna, Amarigna, Anyiwakgna, Arbogigna, Arigna, Arborigna, Bachagna, Basketigna, Benchigna, Bertagna, Bodigna, Brayligna, Burjigna, Benagna, Charigna, Dasenechgna, Dawurogna, Debosgna, Derashigna, Dimegna, Dizigna, Dongigna, Demegna, Felashigna, Fedashigna, Gamogna, Gebatogna, Gedeogna, Gedichogna, Gedoligna, Goffigna, Gumuzigna, Guragiegna, Guagugna, Hadiyigna, Hareriegna, Hamerigna, Irobigna, Kefficho, Kembatigna, Kontigna, Komigna, Konsogna, Koregna, Koygogna, Koyrigna, Kunamigna, Karogna, Kusumegna, Maliegna, Maogna, Marekogna, Mashiligna, Merigna, Me'enigna, Messengogna, Mejengerigna, Mossigna, Mursygna, Murlegna, Naogna, Nuwerigna, Nyangatomigna, Oromigna, Oydigna, Qebenigna, Qechemigna, Qewamigna, Shekacho, Shekogna, Shinashigna, Sidamigna, Shetagna, Somaligna, Surmigna, Shegna, Tigrigna, Timbarogna, Tsemayigna, Welatigna, Wergigna, Yemsagna, Zeysegna, and other.
c. Affar, Agew Awi, Agew Hamyra, Alaba, Amara, Anyiwak, Argoba, Ari, Arborie, Bacha, Basketo, Bench, Berta, Bodi, Brayle, Burji, Bena, Chara, Dasenech, Dawuro, Debase Gewada, Derashe, Dime, Dizi, Donga, Fedashe, Gamo, Gebato, Gedeo, Gedicho, Gidole, Goffa, Gumuz, Guragie, Guagu, Hadiya, Hareri, Hamer, Irob, Kefficho, Kembata, Konta, Komo, Konso, Koro, Koyego, Kunama, Karo, Kusumie, Malie, Mao, Mareko, Mashola, Mere, Meenite, Messengo, Mejenger, Mossiye, Mursi, Murle, Nao, Nuwer, Nyanegatome, Oromo, Oida, Qebena, Qechem, Qewama, Shekecho, Sheko, Shinasha, Sidama, Silte, Somali, Surma, She, Tigrie, Timebaro, Tsemay, Upo, Welaita, Werji, Yem, Zeyese, Zelman, and other.
d. River, lake, pond, harvesting, other.
e. Yield for each type of agricultural product is the quotient of its production and area.

Financial Transparency and Social Accountability under the PBS Program

The *World Development Report 2004: Making Services Work for Poor People* advocated transparency and accountability mechanisms as effective tools for increasing the effectiveness of development projects focused on service delivery. Accordingly, when the Promoting Basic Services (PBS) program started its first phase in 2006, it included a financial transparency and accountability (FTA) component that provided approximately US$11 million to promote the disclosure of budget information to the general public at the local level. It also included a social accountability component that provided about US$6 million to pilot innovative methods of improving citizens' knowledge of their rights and responsibilities with respect to public service delivery. Social accountability activities were implemented through civil society organizations operating where the pilots were located.

The government's initial unfamiliarity with FTA meant that activities were implemented slowly at first, but with additional support, four prototype FTA tools were developed, validated, and disseminated to regions by the end of the program's first phase. These tools included laypersons' guides to the budget process and three templates for disseminating information on the budget and expenditures at local level.[1] The baseline FTA Perceptions Survey was completed in June 2009.

Social accountability activities reached 80 woredas (approximately 12 percent of the country) under the first phase of the program. Activities focused on four basic service sectors: education, health, agriculture, and water and sanitation. The 12 civil society organizations engaged for this work used internationally proven best practices that were new to Ethiopia (the human rights-based approach to development, community score cards, citizen report cards, and participatory budgeting) as well as focus group and interface discussions and participatory planning and monitoring. Although the activities were new to most of the participating organizations, the program achieved its expected outcomes (the adoption of social accountability best practices and the creation of a learning initiative among participating citizens).

Given the potential demonstrated by the FTA and social accountability initiatives in phase one, phase two included substantial resources for their scaling up and institutionalization. Regions started posting their budget appropriations to woredas on their websites. The FTA tools developed in phase one were extended to all regions, translated to regional languages, customized for local conditions in other ways, and disseminated to woredas. Budget literacy training, which had reached 1,500 individuals under the first phase, was expanded to reach 171,017. More generally, FTA was institutionalized in the public finance system. By the end of the second phase, approximately 94 percent of woredas were posting budget and expenditure data using the customized templates, and 53 percent of service facilities on average used the service delivery templates. Forty-three percent of citizens confirmed that woreda officials had sought their views concerning the quality of basic public services. The percentage of citizens reporting knowledge of the woreda budget increased from 13 percent in 2008 to 20 percent in 2011.

The scaled-up social accountability component for phase two was based on findings from an independent evaluation of the pilot. A key difference in the second phase was the shift away from individual service facilities to a sectoral approach that engaged institutions and key actors in the community under a more comprehensive strategy. Activities were piloted in 86 woredas, in collaboration with 45 civil society organizations, with strong results. Community members received training, tools, and other mechanisms to assess service delivery and budget use and develop joint action plans with service users to improve the quality of services.

Building on that foundation, FTA activities (budgeted at almost US$12.5 million) under the third phase of PBS focus on improving the quality of budget and expenditure information provided to the public by refining and simplifying the FTA tools. Continued budget literacy training will expand the awareness of budget processes and issues among citizens and woreda and kebele council members. The program will engage with other sectors to institutionalize FTA by disclosing their budget and service information to citizens. Social accountability activities (budgeted at US$20.5 million under phase three) will be extended to 170 woredas, bringing the total number of woredas with such activities to 344, representing about 4.5 million service users. Impact will be measured through a randomized controlled trial. Existing methodologies will be refined, and new social accountability tools will be carefully considered based on their value added, including participatory planning and budgeting, budget tracking, gender-responsive budgeting, and service charters. Overall, the progression of FTA and social accountability activities under the PBS Program has brought about much greater transparency and accountability in publicly provided basic services.

Note

1. Citizens did not use the tools in the program's first phase, but the groundwork was laid for their use.

The Center and the Periphery in Ethiopia: The Evolution of Today's Federal State

Ethiopia's ethnic composition reflects its turbulent history. During the medieval period, Ethiopia primarily comprised the Tigray, Agaw, and Amhara peoples. Menelik II's ascension to the throne in 1889 initiated a period of territorial expansion, radiating from the province of Shoa in present-day Amhara Region. The areas now known as Beneshangul-Gemuz, Gambella, Southern Nations and Nationalities, Afar, Oromia, and Somali Regions came under the Ethiopian Empire's feudal system. After the Battle of Adwa in 1896 and Europe's recognition of Ethiopian statehood, border treaties were concluded with the surrounding colonial powers, and the modern Ethiopian state was born.

A Legacy of Troubled Relations between the Center and Periphery

Relations between the newly integrated areas and the historic center of the empire were troubled. Menelik sent governors from the center to administer the new territories, but owing to the center's structural weaknesses, successive Ethiopian governments did not effectively control those areas. Exploitive economic policies imposed on those areas led to their visible marginalization and relative underdevelopment, and resulted in limited integration among the border regions within Ethiopia (Mulugeta 2002).

Yet the center tightened its hold over the periphery. According to noted historian Bahru Zewde, "The period after 1941 witnessed the apogee of absolutism. The tentative beginnings in this direction of the pre-1935 years matured into untrammeled autocracy. The power of the state reached a limit unprecedented in Ethiopian history" (Zewde 1991). The revised constitution of 1955 solidified the absolute powers of the emperor, claiming "His dignity…inviolable and His power…indisputable." It also entrenched Amharic as the sole official language and the Ethiopian Orthodox Church as the national religion.

Socialist rule (1974–91) did not diminish the center's hold over the periphery or change the prevailing economic policies of exploitation. Despite the regime's appeal to a socialist ideology, the Derg was identified with an "Amhara suppressor" by the nationalist liberation movements (Weldemariam 2011). Any conduct promoting ethnic individualism, and thereby challenging the state's integrity, was outlawed.

The 1991 victory of the Ethiopian People's Revolutionary Democratic Front over the Derg reversed more than one hundred years of ethnic homogenization. As Christopher Clapham says, "The overthrow of the Mengistu government in May 1991 amounted to more than the collapse of a particular regime. It effectively marked the failure of a project, dating back to Menelik's accession in 1889 of creating a 'modern' and centralized Ethiopian state around a Shoan core" (Clapham 1994).

Ethnic federalism now came to the fore in the Transitional Charter, which allowed the right to self-determination for the country's various "nations and nationalities." Like the Transitional Charter, the new constitution of 1995 recognized the rights of ethnic self-determination up to secession. It also created a federal government with nine regional states divided along ethno-linguistic lines: Tigray; Afar; Amhara; Oromia; Somali; Beneshangul-Gemuz; South Nations, Nationalities, and Peoples; Gambella; and Harari (table C.1).

Table C.1 Ethiopian Regional Population Distribution and Ethnic Composition

Region	Population	Estimated size in square kilometers	Ethnic composition (%)
Tigray	4,316,988	50,078	96.6 Tigray, 1.6 Amhara, 1.8 others
Afar	1,390273	96,707	90.0 Afar, 5.2 Amhara, 1.6 Argobba, 1.2 Tigray, 2.0 others
Amhara	17,221,976	159,173	91.5 Amhara, 4.9 Agaw, 2.6 Oromo, 1.0 others
Oromia	27,158,471	353,006	87.8 Oromo, 7.2 Amhara, 0.9 Gurage, 4.1 others
Somali	4,445,219	279,252	96.2 Somali, 2.3 Oromo, 0.7 Amhara, 0.8 others
SNNP	14,929,548	112,343	19.4 Sidama, 10.6 Welayta, 8.0 Hadiya, 7.5 Gurage, 7.0 Gamo, 5.4 Kafficho, 5.4 Silt'e, 36.7 others
Gambella	307,096	25,802	47.3 Nuer, 21.7 Anyiwak, 8.0 Amhara, 5.2 Opo and Komo, 4.4 Majangir, 13.4 others
Beneshangul-Gemuz	784,354	49,289	25.4 Berta, 21.7 Amhara, 20.9 Gemuz, 13.6 Oromo, 7.7 Shinasha, 4.2 Agaw-Awi, 6.5 others
Harari	183,415	311	56.4 Oromo, 22.8 Amhara, 8.7 Harari, 4.4 Gurage, 3.9 Somali, 1.5 Tigray, 2.5 others

Source: Data from 2007 census conducted by the Central Statistical Agency.
Note: SNNP = Southern Nations, Nationalities, and Peoples (Region).

A primary focus of the new government was economic integration and equitable development. As Meles Zenawi, President of the Federal Democratic Republic of Ethiopia, declared in 1997, "It is only through fast economic growth that is broadly shared by the population that we can hope for sustainable peace. And, therefore, one of the most important pillars of our program is fast economic growth that is equitable and broadly shared among the population" (Meles 1997).

The government adopted a policy of affirmative action toward historically disadvantaged regions, whereby Beneshangul-Gemuz, Gambella, Afar, and Somali would receive preferential treatment in budget allocations and enrollment in higher education. Centralization's legacy is that developing regions are not yet fully integrated into the economy of the Ethiopian state, and few of their residents participate in running the regional administrative structures. The gradual emergence of local administrative officials in the regions, establishment of a more equitable base for development, and better investment in education, health, social and physical infrastructure, and other areas all attest to the positive outcomes of Ethiopia's federalization and affirmative action policy (Adegehe 2009).

The Modern Ethiopian Federal State

Decentralization of political, administrative, and fiscal authority to regional and local governments has been fundamental to the affirmative action strategy. The Government of Ethiopia's strong commitment to decentralization and building a federal state is enshrined in the 1995 Federal Constitution. Decentralization should be seen as a work in progress, in which the underlying institutional arrangements for success are evolving and continue to require focused support.

The first wave of decentralization occurred during the transitional period (1991–94) as state powers devolved to geographically defined ethno-linguistic groups and legislation was passed to create regional and woreda (district) councils. As needed, regions could establish zones as intermediaries between regional and district administrations. In addition to gaining the right to self-determination, the new regional units assumed a range of executive, legislative, and judicial powers. Within their borders, they exercised jurisdiction over social and economic development as well as basic service delivery. Regions were mandated to create the internal institutional arrangements to perform those functions, including a council, executive committee, judicial administration office, public prosecution office, audit office, police and security office, and service and development committee.

Proclamation No. 7/1992 stipulated the sources of revenue for regional governing units, which included tax revenues derived within their jurisdictions, fiscal transfers from the central government, domestic borrowing, and others. The latter category was specified in Proclamation No. 33/1992. Capacity constraints prevented regional governments from performing their revenue-collecting assignments, however, and they remained highly dependent on central government grants to meet their new spending obligations in the social sectors.

Despite these rather elaborate governing arrangements, the new regional governments remained subordinate to the central government. The regional councils were accountable to citizens living within their regional borders, yet legally they were also responsible to the central government's Council of Representatives.

Promulgation of the 1995 Federal Constitution signified another stage in Ethiopia's decentralization. The constitution affirmed the roles and functions of federal versus regional government. The federal government was still charged with a broad range of functions and responsibilities (such as fiscal and monetary policy and international trade), but the regions and woredas gained responsibility for ensuring the delivery of basic services in their respective jurisdictions. The federal government retained authority to set policies and standards in each of the major social service delivery sectors. In 2002, decentralization was extended to the woreda governments, which became largely responsible for service delivery. Woredas receive block grants from their respective regional governments; the size of Woreda Block Grants is determined by formulas set by the regional governments, using methodologies broadly similar to those applied to federal–regional grants.

Decentralization to the woreda level is crucial for achieving an equitable distribution of prosperity. Ethiopian history, sociology, and ethnography all suggest that citizen-state relationships are framed by alternative norms of political culture, power, and state-society relations, which have evolved locally, in the context of historical processes of state formation (World Bank 2013). With decentralization to the woreda level, budgets allocated for local expenditures have increased dramatically. Indicators of human development have similarly improved (net enrollment and vaccination rates are just two examples). Decentralization and affirmative action are mitigating the effects of economic policies that prevailed for more than a century, resulting in more broadly shared economic prosperity.

Detailed Regression Results

Table D.1 Stage 1: Education—Linear Regression Association of Per Capita Education Expenditures with Net Enrollment Rate

Linear Regression
Dependent variable: Net Enrollment Rate

Independent variables:	OLS
Yearly expenditure per capita in Education	0.045
	(0.0091)
Yearly regional per capita Capital Expenditure	174.331
	(1,580.6640)
Percentage of rural population	−12.283*
	(6.7861)
Ethnicity controls	
Nuwer	−7.387
	(24.1886)
Anyiwak	−11.089
	(27.8701)
Gumuz	−16.048
	(24.4713)
Konso	−48.182
	(44.7173)
Hist. Adv.	−0.967
	(7.2677)
Somali	−62.222***
	(10.1186)
Affar	77.755***
	(11.4409)
Other Small	−13.178
	(8.5432)

table continues next page

Table D.1 Stage 1: Education—Linear Regression Association of Per Capita Education Expenditures with Net Enrollment Rate (continued)

Time controls	
T zero	−3.548***
	(1.2457)
T one	−4.863***
	(0.9834)
T two	−0.301
	(0.6894)
T three	Omitted
Constant	104.449***
	(9.4504)

Note: Cross-time pooled regressions with robust standard errors; standard errors in parentheses; * , **, *** = coefficients significant at the 10 percent, 5 percent and 1 percent levels. OLS = ordinary least squares.

Table D.2 Stage 1: Education—Quadratic Regression Association of Per Capita Education Expenditures with Net Enrollment Rate

Quadratic Regression

Dependent variable: Net Enrollment Rate

Independent variables:	OLS
Yearly expenditure per capita in Education	0.025
	(0.0223)
Yearly expenditure per capita in Education Squared	−0.00005
	(0.00003)
Yearly regional per capita Capital Expenditure	55.277
	(1,583.27)
Percentage of rural population	−10.394
	(6.8810)
Ethnicity controls	
Nuwer	−8.569
	(24.1212)
Anyiwak	−13.453
	(27.8232)
Gumuz	−18.196
	(24.4323)
Konso	−48.041
	(44.5685)
Hist. Adv.	−1.193
	(7.2454)
Somali	−61.075***
	(10.1151)
Affar	−77.279***
	(11.4079)
Other Small	−13.489
	(8.5172)

table continues next page

Table D.2 Stage 1: Education—Quadratic Regression Association of Per Capita Education Expenditures with Net Enrollment Rate *(continued)*

Time controls	
T zero	−2.438*
	(1.4520)
T one	−3.952***
	(1.1585)
T two	0.087
	(0.7375)
T three	Omitted
Constant	100.071***
	(9.8686)

Note: Cross-time pooled regressions with robust standard errors; standard errors in parentheses; * , **, *** = coefficients significant at the 10 percent, 5 percent and 1 percent levels. OLS = ordinary least squares.

Table D.3 Stage 1: Education—Log Linear Regression Association of Per Capita Education Expenditures with Net Enrollment Rate

Log Linear Regression

Dependent variable: Log Net Enrollment Rate

Independent variables:	OLS
Log yearly expenditure per capita in Education	0.276***
	(0.0280)
Log yearly regional per capita Capital Expenditure	0.040
	(0.0293)
Percentage of rural population	0.110
	(0.0830)
Ethnicity controls	
Nuwer	−0.042
	(0.2949)
Anyiwak	−0.545*
	(0.3428)
Gumuz	−0.130
	(0.3081)
Konso	−0.467
	(0.5273)
Hist. Adv.	0.004
	(0.0861)
Somali	−0.845***
	(0.1267)
Affar	−1.506***
	(0.1490)
Other Small	−0.132
	(0.0120)

table continues next page

Table D.3 Stage 1: Education—Log Linear Regression Association of Per Capita Education Expenditures with Net Enrollment Rate *(continued)*

Time controls	
T zero	0.144***
	(0.0266)
T one	0.091***
	(0.0203)
T two	0.062
	(0.0120)
T three	Omitted
Constant	3.263***
	(0.2725)

Note: Cross-time pooled regressions with robust standard errors; standard errors in parentheses; * , **, *** = coefficients significant at the 10 percent, 5 percent and 1 percent levels. OLS = ordinary least squares.

Table D.4 Stage 1: Education—Linear Regression Association of Per Capita Education Expenditures with Pupil-Teacher Ratio

Linear Regression
Dependent variable: Pupil-Teacher Ratio

Independent variables:	OLS
Yearly expenditure per capita in Education	−0.024
	(0.0199)
Yearly regional per capita Capital Expenditure	8,000.899***
	(2,800.951)
Percentage of rural population	15.676
	(4.7215)
Ethnicity controls	
Nuwer	−3.408
	(13.6348)
Anyiwak	−32.619*
	(17.6828)
Gumuz	−21.557
	(14.7049)
Konso	−18.551
	(26.2358)
Hist. Adv.	−15.588***
	(4.1635)
Somali	39.245***
	(6.1928)
Affar	−26.338***
	(7.1540)
Other Small	−7.671
	(4.7664)

table continues next page

Table D.4 Stage 1: Education—Linear Regression Association of Per Capita Education Expenditures with Pupil-Teacher Ratio *(continued)*

Time controls	
T zero	6.381**
	(2.6909)
T one	1.990
	(2.1899)
T two	4.038**
	(1.6336)
T three	Omitted
Constant	43.085***
	(8.1009)

Note: Cross-time pooled regressions with robust standard errors; standard errors in parentheses; *, **, *** = coefficients significant at the 10 percent, 5 percent and 1 percent levels. OLS = ordinary least squares.

Table D.5 Stage 1: Education—Quadratic Regression Association of Per Capita Education Expenditures with Pupil-Teacher Ratio

Quadratic Regression
Dependent variable: Pupil-Teacher Ratio

Independent variables:	OLS
Yearly expenditure per capita in Education	−0.110***
	(0.0403)
Yearly expenditure per capita in Education Squared	0.0002**
	(0.00006)
Yearly regional per capita Capital Expenditure	7,472.043***
	(2,805.786)
Percentage of rural population	12.328**
	(4.9101)
Ethnicity controls	
Nuwer	−0.908
	(13.6528)
Anyiwak	−34.057**
	(17.6673)
Gumuz	−17.969
	(14.7562)
Konso	−18.807
	(26.1966)
Hist. Adv.	−14.821***
	(4.1692)
Somali	35.936***
	(6.3310)

table continues next page

Table D.5 Stage 1: Education—Quadratic Regression Association of Per Capita Education Expenditures with Pupil-Teacher Ratio *(continued)*

Affar	−28.423***
	(7.1947)
Other Small	−7.151
	(4.7640)
Time controls	
T zero	3.476
	(2.9395)
T one	−0.288
	(2.3785)
T two	3.067*
	(1.6798)
T three	Omitted
Constant	53.924***
	(9.2286)

Note: Cross-time pooled regressions with robust standard errors; standard errors in parentheses; *, **, *** = coefficients significant at the 10 percent, 5 percent and 1 percent levels. OLS = ordinary least squares.

Table D.6 Stage 1: Education—Log Linear Regression Association of Per Capita Education Expenditures with Pupil-Teacher Ratio

Log Linear Regression
Dependent variable: Pupil-Teacher Ratio

Independent variables:	OLS
Log yearly expenditure per capita in Education	−0.223***
	(0.0203)
Log yearly regional per capita Capital Expenditure	0.063***
	(0.0158)
Percentage of rural population	0.202***
	(0.0363)
Ethnicity controls	
Nuwer	0.234
	(0.1176)
Anyiwak	−0.600***
	(0.1424)
Gumuz	−0.252
	(0.1299)
Konso	−0.315
	(0.2126)
Hist. Adv.	−0.227***
	(0.0329)
Somali	0.146**
	(0.0528)

table continues next page

Table D.6   Stage 1: Education—Log Linear Regression Association of Per Capita Education Expenditures with Pupil-Teacher Ratio (continued)

Affar	−0.556***
	(0.0658)
Other Small	−0.129***
	(0.0389)
Time controls	
T zero	−0.044
	(0.0193)
T one	−0.096***
	(0.0153)
T two	0.007
	(0.0099)
T three	Omitted
Constant	5.434***
	(0.1460)

Note: Cross-time pooled regressions with robust standard errors; standard errors in parentheses; *, **, *** = coefficients significant at the 10 percent, 5 percent and 1 percent levels. OLS = ordinary least squares.

Table D.7   Stage 1: Health—Linear Regression Association of Per Capita Health Expenditures with Penta3 Vaccination Rate

Linear Regression
Dependent variable: Penta3 Vaccination Rate

Independent variables:	OLS
Yearly expenditure per capita in Health	−0.063***
	(0.0233)
Yearly regional per capita Capital Expenditure	−1,447.151
	(1,315.3060)
Percentage of rural population	8.677***
	(1.8676)
Ethnicity controls	
Nuwer	−64.966***
	(6.4810)
Anyiwak	−53.901***
	(8.3259)
Gumuz	−44.426***
	(7.3255)
Konso	−50.230**
	(24.1339)
Hist. Adv.	−9.565***
	(2.0970)
Somali	−51.458***
	(2.7817)

table continues next page

Table D.7 Stage 1: Health—Log Linear Regression Association of Per Capita Health Expenditures with Penta3 Vaccination Rate *(continued)*

Affar	−47.295***
	(3.2447)
Other Small	−13.755***
	(2.4127)
Time controls	
T zero	−9.362***
	(1.2211)
T one	−3.007**
	(1.2684)
T two	−6.915***
	(0.8858)
T three	Omitted
Constant	91.697***
	(3.1549)

Note: Cross-time pooled regressions with robust standard errors; standard errors in parentheses; *, **, *** = coefficients significant at the 10 percent, 5 percent and 1 percent levels. OLS = ordinary least squares.

Table D.8 Stage 1: Health—Quadratic Regression Association of Per Capita Health Expenditures with Penta3 Vaccination Rate

Quadratic Regression
Dependent variable: Penta3 Vaccination Rate

Independent variables:	OLS
Yearly expenditure per capita in Health	−0.122***
	(0.0395)
Yearly expenditure per capita in Health Squared	0.0003*
	(0.0001)
Yearly regional per capita Capital Expenditure	−1431.498
	(1,315.529)
Percentage of rural population	8.152***
	(1.8899)
Ethnicity controls	
Nuwer	−64.123***
	(6.4999)
Anyiwak	−55.78***
	(8.3911)
Gumuz	−43.354***
	(7.3510)
Konso	−49.085**
	(24.1561)
Hist. Adv.	−9.581***
	(2.0974)

table continues next page

Table D.8 Stage 1: Health—Quadratic Regression Association of Per Capita Health Expenditures with Penta3 Vaccination Rate (continued)

Somali	−51.333***
	(2.7833)
Affar	−46.810***
	(3.2567)
Other Small	−13.546***
	(2.4160)
Time controls	
T zero	−9.963***
	(1.2633)
T one	−3.535***
	(1.2994)
T two	−7.166***
	(0.8955)
T three	Omitted
Constant	93.646***
	(3.3278)

Note: Cross-time pooled regressions with robust standard errors; standard errors in parentheses; * , **, *** = coefficients significant at the 10 percent, 5 percent and 1 percent levels. OLS = ordinary least squares.

Table D.9 Stage 1: Health—Log Linear Regression Association of Per Capita Health Expenditures with Penta3 Vaccination Rate

Log Linear Regression
Dependent variable: Penta3 Vaccination Rate

Independent variables:	OLS
Log yearly expenditure per capita in Health	−0.058**
	(0.0276)
Log yearly regional per capita Capital Expenditure	−0.003
	(0.0262)
Percentage of rural population	0.182***
	(0.0512)
Ethnicity controls	
Nuwer	−1.919***
	(0.1910)
Anyiwak	−1.018***
	(0.2379)
Gumuz	−0.701***
	(0.2067)
Konso	−0.626
	(0.6551)
Hist. Adv.	−0.141**
	(0.0595)

table continues next page

Table D.9 Stage 1: Health—Log Linear Regression Association of Per Capita Health Expenditures with Penta3 Vaccination Rate *(continued)*

Somali	−1.048***
	(0.0796)
Affar	−1.026***
	(0.0843)
Other Small	−0.220***
	(0.0697)
Time controls	
T zero	−0.170***
	(0.0404)
T one	−0.095**
	(0.0428)
T two	−0.131 ***
	(0.0296)
T three	Omitted
Constant	4.613***
	(0.2042)

Note: Cross-time pooled regressions with robust standard errors; standard errors in parentheses; *, **, *** = coefficients significant at the 10 percent, 5 percent and 1 percent levels. OLS = ordinary least squares.

Table D.10 Stage 1: Health—Linear Regression Association of Per Capita Health Expenditures with Antenatal Care

Linear Regression
Dependent variable: Antenatal Care

Independent variables:	OLS
Yearly expenditure per capita in Health	0.026
	(0.0313)
Yearly regional per capita Capital Expenditure	−249.548
	(1,711.0580)
Percentage of rural population	−10.849***
	(2.4200)
Ethnicity controls	
Nuwer	−56.384***
	(8.5451)
Anyiwak	−44.982***
	(10.2385)
Gumuz	−59.973***
	(9.1047)
Konso	−42.666
	(30.2839)
Hist. Adv.	−13.034***
	(2.5008)

table continues next page

Table D.10 Stage 1: Health—Linear Regression Association of Per Capita Health Expenditures with Antenatal Care *(continued)*

Somali	−41.722***
	(3.4255)
Affar	−59.354***
	(4.0043)
Other Small	−13.486***
	(2.8967)
Time controls	
T zero	−13.198***
	(1.6319)
T one	−6.886***
	(1.6671)
T two	−4.589***
	(1.2176)
T three	Omitted
Constant	96.300***
	(4.0269)

Note: Cross-time pooled regressions with robust standard errors; standard errors in parentheses; *, **, *** = coefficients significant at the 10 percent, 5 percent and 1 percent levels. OLS = ordinary least squares.

Table D.11 Stage 1: Health—Quadratic Regression Association of Per Capita Health Expenditures with Antenatal Care

Quadratic Regression
Dependent variable: Antenatal Care

Independent variables:	OLS
Yearly expenditure per capita in Health	0.086
	(0.0532)
Yearly expenditure per capita in Health Squared	−0.0003
	(0.0002)
Yearly regional per capita Capital Expenditure	−238.134
	(1,711.9540)
Percentage of rural population	−10.305***
	(2.4525)
Ethnicity controls	
Nuwer	−57.340***
	(8.5779)
Anyiwak	−43.322***
	(10.3145)
Gumuz	−61.090***
	(9.1462)
Konso	−43.918
	(30.3276)

table continues next page

Table D.11 Stage 1: Health—Quadratic Regression Association of Per Capita Health Expenditures with Antenatal Care *(continued)*

Hist. Adv.	−13.080***
	(2.5029)
Somali	−41.852***
	(3.4293)
Affar	−59.895***
	(4.0262)
Other Small	−13.747***
	(2.9050)
Time controls	
T zero	−12.542***
	(1.6965)
T one	−6.326***
	(1.7131)
T two	−4.323***
	(1.2316)
T three	Omitted
Constant	94.305***
	(4.2712)

Note: Cross-time pooled regressions with robust standard errors; standard errors in parentheses; *, **, *** = coefficients significant at the 10 percent, 5 percent and 1 percent levels. OLS = ordinary least squares.

Table D.12 Stage 1: Health—Log Linear Regression Association of Per Capita Health Expenditures with Antenatal Care

Log Linear Regression
Dependent variable: Antenatal Care

Independent variables:	OLS
Log yearly expenditure per capita in Health	0.086**
	(0.0347)
Log yearly regional per capita Capital Expenditure	−0.021
	(0.0330)
Percentage of rural population	−0.016
	(0.0671)
Ethnicity controls	
Nuwer	−2.710***
	(0.2509)
Anyiwak	−0.718***
	(0.2905)
Gumuz	−1.1760***
	(0.2727)
Konso	−0.635
	(0.8460)

table continues next page

Table D.12 Stage 1: Health—Log Linear Regression Association of Per Capita Health Expenditures with Antenatal Care (continued)

Hist. Adv.	−0.178**
	(0.0683)
Somali	−0.852***
	(0.1017)
Affar	−1.768***
	(0.1280)
Other Small	−0.230***
	(0.0815)
Time controls	
T zero	−0.197***
	(0.0485)
T one	−0.134***
	(0.0485)
T two	−0.107 ***
	(0.0339)
T three	Omitted
Constant	4.330***
	(0.1601)

Note: Cross-time pooled regressions with robust standard errors; standard errors in parentheses; * , **, *** = coefficients significant at the 10 percent, 5 percent and 1 percent levels. OLS = ordinary least squares.

Table D.13 Stage 1: Health—Linear Regression Association of Per Capita Health Expenditures with Contraceptive Acceptance Rate

Linear Regression
Dependent variable: Contraceptive Acceptance rate

Independent variables:	*OLS*
Yearly expenditure per capita in Health	−0.052*
	(0.0287)
Yearly regional per capita Capital Expenditure	−1,371.507
	(1,583.1580)
Percentage of rural population	−11.900***
	(2.2773)
Ethnicity controls	
Nuwer	−64.900***
	(7.8045)
Anyiwak	−45.951***
	(9.5779)
Gumuz	−57.212***
	(8.3646)
Konso	−10.295
	(28.6759)

table continues next page

Table D.13 Stage 1: Health—Linear Regression Association of Per Capita Health Expenditures with Contraceptive Acceptance Rate (continued)

Hist. Adv.	−5.363**
	(2.3429)
Somali	−61.431***
	(3.302)
Affar	−53.855***
	(3.7462)
Other Small	−12.126***
	(2.7181)
Time controls	
T zero	−14.651***
	(1.4963)
T one	−8.743***
	(1.4947)
T two	−3.260***
	(1.0739)
T three	Omitted
Constant	83.648***
	(3.7609)

Note: Cross-time pooled regressions with robust standard errors; standard errors in parentheses; *, **, *** = coefficients significant at the 10 percent, 5 percent and 1 percent levels. OLS = ordinary least squares.

Table D.14 Stage 1: Health—Quadratic Regression Association of Per Capita Health Expenditures with Contraceptive Acceptance Rate

Quadratic Regression
Dependent variable: Contraceptive Acceptance rate

Independent variables:	OLS
Yearly expenditure per capita in Health	−0.012
	(0.0493)
Yearly expenditure per capita in Health Squared	−0.00023
	(0.0002)
Yearly regional per capita Capital Expenditure	−1,351.924
	(1,583.894)
Percentage of rural population	−11.527***
	(2.3092)
Ethnicity controls	
Nuwer	65.492***
	(7.8317)
Anyiwak	−45.000***
	(9.6311)
Gumuz	−57.931***
	(8.4008)

table continues next page

Table D.14 Stage 1: Health—Quadratic Regression Association of Per Capita Health Expenditures with Contraceptive Acceptance Rate (continued)

Konso	−11.154
	(28.7083)
Hist. Adv.	−5.396**
	(2.3444)
Somali	−61.430***
	(3.3037)
Affar	−54.207***
	(3.7654)
Other Small	−12.297***
	(2.7251)
Time controls	
T zero	−14.187***
	(1.5666)
T one	−8.350***
	(1.5451)
T two	−3.075***
	(1.0896)
T three	Omitted
Constant	82.290***
	(4.0021)

Note: Cross-time pooled regressions with robust standard errors; standard errors in parentheses; * , **, *** = coefficients significant at the 10 percent, 5 percent and 1 percent levels. OLS = ordinary least squares.

Table D.15 Stage 1: Health—Log Linear Regression Association of Per Capita Health Expenditures with Contraceptive Acceptance Rate

Log Linear Regression
Dependent variable: Contraceptive Acceptance rate

Independent variables:	OLS
Log yearly expenditure per capita in Health	−0.006
	(0.0410)
Log yearly regional per capita Capital Expenditure	−0.056
	(0.0390)
Percentage of rural population	−0.136
	(0.0796)
Ethnicity controls	
Nuwer	−4.864***
	(0.2766)
Anyiwak	−1.567***
	(0.3427)
Gumuz	−1.552***
	(0.3164)

table continues next page

Table D.15 Stage 1: Health—Log Linear Regression Association of Per Capita Health Expenditures with Contraceptive Acceptance Rate *(continued)*

Konso	−0.232
	(1.0094)
Hist. Adv.	−0.116
	(0.0805)
Somali	−2.671***
	(0.1225)
Affar	−1.971***
	(0.1507)
Other Small	−0.309***
	(0.0963)
Time controls	
T zero	−0.308***
	(0.0561)
T one	−0.221***
	(0.0559)
T two	−0.0058**
	(0.0371)
T three	Omitted
Constant	4.744***
	(0.3058)

Note: Cross-time pooled regressions with robust standard errors; standard errors in parentheses; *, **, *** = coefficients significant at the 10 percent, 5 percent and 1 percent levels. OLS = ordinary least squares.

Table D. 16 Stage 1: Health—Linear Regression Association of Per Capita Health Expenditures with Delivery by Skilled Birth Attendant

Linear Regression
Dependent variable: Delivery by Skilled Birth Attendant

Independent variables:	OLS
Yearly expenditure per capita in Health	0.066***
	(0.0287)
Yearly regional per capita Capital Expenditure	328.600
	(1,211.0980)
Percentage of rural population	−22.745***
	(1.7421)
Ethnicity controls	
Nuwer	−15.830***
	(5.9881)
Anyiwak	−19.264***
	(7.4207)
Gumuz	−17.340***
	(6.2405)

table continues next page

Table D. 16 Stage 1: Health—Linear Regression Association of Per Capita Health Expenditures with Delivery by Skilled Birth Attendant (continued)

Konso	−3.805
	(20.9835)
Hist. Adv.	−4.326**
	(1.7805)
Somali	−10.021***
	(2.5271)
Affar	−9.327***
	(2.8013)
Other Small	−5.143**
	(2.0568)
Time controls	
T zero	−3.308***
	(1.1900)
T one	−4.626***
	(1.2333)
T two	1.012
	(0.9168)
T three	Omitted
Constant	40.980***
	(2.8922)

Note: Cross-time pooled regressions with robust standard errors; standard errors in parentheses; *, **, *** = coefficients significant at the 10 percent, 5 percent and 1 percent levels. OLS = ordinary least squares.

Table D.17 Stage 1: Health—Quadratic Regression Association of Per Capita Health Expenditures with Delivery by Skilled Birth Attendant

Quadratic Regression
Dependent variable: Delivery by Skilled Birth Attendant

Independent variables:	OLS
Yearly expenditure per capita in Health	0.068*
	(0.0389)
Yearly expenditure per capita in Health Squared	−0.00001
	(0.0001)
Yearly regional per capita Capital Expenditure	330.274
	(1,211.889)
Percentage of rural population	−22.726***
	(1.7685)
Ethnicity controls	
Nuwer	−15.862***
	(6.0100)
Anyiwak	−19.204**
	(7.4858)

table continues next page

Table D.17   Stage 1: Health—Quadratic Regression Association of Per Capita Health Expenditures with Delivery by Skilled Birth Attendant *(continued)*

Gumuz	−17.374***
	(6.2652)
Konso	−3.847
	(21.0059)
Hist. Adv.	−4.327**
	(1.7815)
Somali	−10.024***
	(2.5288)
Affar	−9.344***
	(2.8147)
Other Small	−5.152**
	(2.0616)
Time controls	
T zero	−3.285***
	(1.2422)
T one	−4.607***
	(1.2694)
T two	1.021
	(0.9270)
T three	Omitted
Constant	40.911***
	(3.0919)

Note: Cross-time pooled regressions with robust standard errors; standard errors in parentheses; *, **, *** = coefficients significant at the 10 percent, 5 percent and 1 percent levels. OLS = ordinary least squares.

Table D.18   Stage 1: Health—Log Linear Regression Association of Per Capita Health Expenditures with Delivery by Skilled Birth Attendant

Log Linear Regression
Dependent variable: Delivery by Skilled Birth Attendant

Independent variables:	OLS
Log yearly expenditure per capita in Health	0.267***
	(0.0747)
Log yearly regional per capita Capital Expenditure	−0.071
	(0.0698)
Percentage of rural population	−0.720***
	(0.1456)
Ethnicity controls	
Nuwer	−2.329***
	(0.5238)
Anyiwak	−1.914***
	(0.6249)

table continues next page

Table D.18 Stage 1: Health—Log Linear Regression Association of Per Capita Health Expenditures with Delivery by Skilled Birth Attendant (continued)

Gumuz	−0.777**
	(0.5637)
Konso	−0.372
	(1.7985)
Hist. Adv.	0.033
	(0.1450)
Somali	−0.620***
	(0.2224)
Affar	−1.310***
	(0.2378)
Other Small	−1.106
	(0.1726)
Time controls	
T zero	−0.027
	(0.0981)
T one	−0.362***
	(0.0976)
T two	−0.042
	(0.0700)
T three	Omitted
Constant	2.818***
	(0.5497)

Note: Probit regressions with robust standard errors in parentheses; Predicted probabilities with unconditional standard errors in parentheses; *, **, *** = coefficients significant at the 10 percent, 5 percent and 1 percent levels. OLS = ordinary least squares.

Table D.19 Stage 1: Agriculture—Log Linear Regression Association of Per Capita Agriculture Expenditures with Cereal Yield

Log Linear Regression
Dependent variable: Cereal Yield

Independent variables:	OLS
Log yearly expenditure per capita in Agriculture	0.128***
	(0. 0489)
Percentage of rural population	−0.414*
	(0.2205)
Rainfall controls	
Average rainfall	0.000
	(0.0008)
Deviation from average rainfall	0.001**
	(0.0007)
Deviation from average rainfall (lagged)	0.002***
	(0.0007)

table continues next page

Table D.19 Stage 1: Agriculture—Log Linear Regression Association of per Capita Agriculture expenditures with Cereal Yield *(continued)*

Regional dummies	
Tigray	4.576
	(9.0103)
Afar	3.544
	(8.5370)
Amhara	3.522
	(8.9863)
Oromia	3.951
	(8.9503)
Somali	11.307
	(9.2046)
Beneshangul Gemuz	17.258
	(18.0467)
SNNP	3.502
	(8.9883)
Gambella	Omitted
Regional dummies × average rainfall	
Tigray × average rainfall	0.000
	(0.0009)
Afar × average rainfall	Omitted
Amhara × average rainfall	0.000
	(0.0009)
Oromia × average rainfall	0.000
	(0.0008)
Somali × average rainfall	−0.010***
	(0.0027)
Beneshangul Gemuz × average rainfall	−0.011
	(0.0128)
SNNP × average rainfall	0.000
	(0.0008)
Gambella × average rainfall	Omitted
Regional dummies × Poverty rate	
Tigray × Poverty rate	−0.020
	(0.0182)
Afar × Poverty rate	Omitted
Amhara × Poverty rate	−0.003
	(0.0058)
Oromia × Poverty rate	0.002
	(0.0063)
Somali × Poverty rate	−0.078***
	(0.0200)

table continues next page

Table D.19 Stage 1: Agriculture—Log Linear Regression Association of Per Capita Agriculture Expenditures with Pulses Yield *(continued)*

Beneshangul Gemuz × Poverty rate	−0.036
	(0.0438)
SNNP × Poverty rate	0.000
	(0.0025)
Gambella × Poverty rate	0.102
	(0.2498)
Constant	−1.510
	(8.9315)

Note: Cross-time pooled regressions with robust standard errors; standard errors in parentheses; * , **, *** = coefficients significant at the 10 percent, 5 percent and 1 percent levels. Dire Dawa and Hara omitted due to small scale of agriculture in these regions. OLS = ordinary least squares; SNNP = Southern Nations, Nationalities, and Peoples (Region).

Table D.20 Stage 1: Agriculture—Log Linear Regression Association of Per Capita Agriculture Expenditures with Pulses Yield

Log Linear Regression
Dependent variable: Pulses Yield

Independent variables:	OLS
Log yearly expenditure per capita in Agriculture	−0.020
	(0.0645)
Percentage of rural population	0.105
	(0.2456)
Rainfall controls	
Average rainfall	0.001
	(0.0014)
Deviation from average rainfall	0.001
	(0.0010)
Deviation from average rainfall (lagged)	0.001
	(0.0010)
Regional dummies	
Tigray	3.165
	(2.126)
Afar	0.918
	(1.1132)
Amhara	2.115
	(1.9126)
Oromia	3.184*
	(1.8845)
Somali	3.569
	(3.0569)
Beneshangul Gemuz	39.151*
	(20.4730)

table continues next page

Table D.20 Stage 1: Agriculture—Log Linear Regression Association of Per Capita Agriculture Expenditures with Pulses Yield *(continued)*

SNNP	2.462
	(1.9117)
Gambella	Omitted
Regional dummies × average rainfall	
Tigray × average rainfall	−0.001
	(0.0015)
Afar × average rainfall	Omitted
Amhara × average rainfall	0.000
	(0.0014)
Oromia × average rainfall	−0.001
	(0.0014)
Somali × average rainfall	−0.002
	(0.0036)
Beneshangul Gemuz × average rainfall	−0.030*
	(0.0166)
SNNP × average rainfall	−0.001
	(0.0014)
Gambella × average rainfall	Omitted
Regional dummies × Poverty rate	
Tigray × Poverty rate	−0.012
	(0.0196)
Afar × Poverty rate	Omitted
Amhara × Poverty rate	−0.008
	(0.0063)
Oromia × Poverty rate	−0.010
	(0.0070)
Somali × Poverty rate	−0.027
	(0.0265)
Beneshangul Gemuz × Poverty rate	−0.126**
	(0.0563)
SNNP × Poverty rate	0.002
	(0.0027)
Gambella × Poverty rate	Omitted
Constant	−0.213
	(1.8785)

Note: Cross-time pooled regressions with robust standard errors; standard errors in parentheses; *, **, *** = coefficients significant at the 10 percent, 5 percent and 1 percent levels. OLS = ordinary least squares; SNNP =Southern Nations, Nationalities, and Peoples (Region). Dire Dawa and Hara omitted due to small scale of agriculture in these regions

Table D.21 Stage 1: Agriculture—Log Linear Regression Association of Per Capita Agriculture Expenditures with Root Crop Yield

Log Linear Regression
Dependent variable: Root Crop Yield

Independent variables:	OLS
Log yearly expenditure per capita in Agriculture	0.320
	(0.2266)
Percentage of rural population	−0.082
	(0.7218)
Rainfall controls	
Average rainfall	0.000
	(0.0032)
Deviation from average rainfall	0.002
	(0.0039)
Deviation from average rainfall (lagged)	0.010
	(0.0039)
Regional dummies	
Tigray	0.739
	(5.2598)
Afar	Omitted
Amhara	0.314
	(4.4270)
Oromia	0.579
	(4.4138)
Somali	−1.041
	(5.5139)
Beneshangul Gemuz	4.842
	(43.2237)
SNNP	0.626
	(4.4447)
Gambella	Omitted
Regional dummies × average rainfall	
Tigray × average rainfall	0.000
	(0.0036)
Afar × average rainfall	Omitted
Amhara × average rainfall	0.000
	(0.0033)
Oromia × average rainfall	0.000
	(0.0033)
Somali × average rainfall	0.003
	(0.0069)
Beneshangul Gemuz × average rainfall	−0.003
	(0.0351)

table continues next page

Table D.21 Stage 1: Agriculture—Log Linear Regression Association of Per Capita Agriculture Expenditures with Root Crop Yield (continued)

SNNP × average rainfall	0.000
	(0.0033)
Gambella × average rainfall	Omitted
Regional dummies × Poverty rate	
Tigray × Poverty rate	0.012
	(0.0618)
Afar × Poverty rate	Omitted
Amhara × Poverty rate	−0.008
	(0.0170)
Oromia × Poverty rate	−0.009
	(0.0211)
Somali × Poverty rate	Omitted
Beneshangul Gemuz × Poverty rate	−0.006
	(0.1203)
SNNP × Poverty rate	−0.016**
	(0.0074)
Gambella × Poverty rate	Omitted
Constant	2.431
	(4.5185)

Note: Cross-time pooled regressions with robust standard errors; standard errors in parentheses; * , **, *** = coefficients significant at the 10 percent, 5 percent and 1 percent levels. OLS = ordinary least squares; SNNP = Southern Nations, Nationalities, and Peoples (Region). Dire Dawa and Hara omitted due to small scale of agriculture in these regions.

Table D.22 Stage 1: Agriculture—Log Linear Regression Association of Per Capita Agriculture Expenditures with Vegetable Yield

Log Linear Regression
Dependent variable: Vegetable Yield

Independent variables:	OLS
Log yearly expenditure per capita in Agriculture	0.582***
	(0.1330)
Percentage of rural population	−0.110
	(0.5548)
Rainfall controls	
Average rainfall	0.001
	(0.0021)
Deviation from average rainfall	0.001
	(0.0020)
Deviation from average rainfall (lagged)	−0.003
	(0.0021)
Regional dummies	
Tigray	32.703
	(22.4893)
Afar	34.322
	(22.5041)
Amhara	32.568
	(22.4326)
Oromia	33.773
	(22.3465)
Somali	10.227
	(22.9840)
Beneshangul Gemuz	35.983
	(43.4964)
SNNP	31.791
	(22.4365)
Gambella	Omitted
Regional dummies × average rainfall	
Tigray × average rainfall	−0.002
	(0.0024)
Afar × average rainfall	−0.005
	(0.0042)
Amhara × average rainfall	−0.002
	(0.0022)
Oromia × average rainfall	−0.002
	(0.0021)
Somali × average rainfall	0.031***
	(0.0067)

table continues next page

Table D.22 Stage 1: Agriculture—Log Linear Regression Association of Per Capita Agriculture Expenditures with Vegetable Yield *(continued)*

Beneshangul Gemuz × average rainfall	−0.005
	(0.0306)
SNNP × average rainfall	0.001
	(0.0021)
Gambella × average rainfall	Omitted
Regional dummies × Poverty rate	
Tigray × Poverty rate	0.004
	(0.0618)
Afar × Poverty rate	Omitted
Amhara × Poverty rate	−0.003
	(0.0145)
Oromia × Poverty rate	−0.034**
	(0.0159)
Somali × Poverty rate	0.185***
	(0.0490)
Beneshangul Gemuz × Poverty rate	−0.036
	(0.1049)
SNNP × Poverty rate	−0.004
	(0.0064)
Gambella × Poverty rate	0.919
	(0.6237)
Constant	−29.575
	(22.3062)

Note: Cross-time pooled regressions with robust standard errors; standard errors in parentheses; *, **, *** = coefficients significant at the 10 percent, 5 percent and 1 percent levels. OLS = ordinary least squares; SNNP = Southern Nations, Nationalities, and Peoples (Region). Dire Dawa and Hara omitted due to small scale of agriculture in these regions

Table D.23 Stage 1: Agriculture—Log Linear Regression Association of Per Capita Agriculture Expenditures with Oil Seeds Yield

Log Linear Regression
Dependent variable: Oil seeds Yield

Independent variables:	OLS
Log yearly expenditure per capita in Agriculture	−0.118
	(0.1899)
Percentage of rural population	−0.229
	(0.6220)
Rainfall controls	
Average rainfall	−0.008***
	(0.0024)
Deviation from average rainfall	−0.001
	(0.0034)
Deviation from average rainfall (lagged)	−0.001
	(0.0036)
Regional dummies	
Tigray	−43.523*
	(25.2816)
Afar	−38.156
	(24.0540)
Amhara	−42.608*
	(25.2609)
Oromia	−42.904*
	(25.1993)
Somali	−41.315*
	(24.3306)
Beneshangul Gemuz	−52.981
	(44.3822)
SNNP	−44.061*
	(25.2585)
Gambella	Omitted
Regional dummies × average rainfall	
Tigray × average rainfal	0.008***
	(0.0027)
Afar × average rainfall	Omitted
Amhara × average rainfall	0.008***
	(0.0025)
Oromia × average rainfall	0.008***
	(0.0025)
Somali × average rainfall	Omitted
Beneshangul Gemuz × average rainfall	0.017***
	(0.0025)

table continues next page

Table D.23 Stage 1: Agriculture—Log Linear Regression Association of Per Capita Agriculture Expenditures with Oil Seeds Yield (continued)

SNNP × average rainfall	0.009***
	(0.0025)
Gambella × average rainfall	Omitted
Regional dummies × Poverty rate	
Tigray × Poverty rate	0.017
	(0.0450)
Afar × Poverty rate	Omitted
Amhara × Poverty rate	0.001
	(0.0144)
Oromia × Poverty rate	0.007
	(0.0186)
Somali × Poverty rate	Omitted
Beneshangul Gemuz × Poverty rate	0.012
	(0.1041)
SNNP × Poverty rate	0.000
	(0.7084)
Gambella × Poverty rate	−1.044*
	(0.7084)
Constant	45.731*
	(25.1903)

Note: Cross-time pooled regressions with robust standard errors; standard errors in parentheses; * , **, *** = coefficients significant at the 10 percent, 5 percent and 1 percent levels. OLS = ordinary least squares; SNNP = Southern Nations, Nationalities, and Peoples (Region). Dire Dawa and Hara omitted due to small scale of agriculture in these regions

Table D.24 Stage 1: Agriculture—Log Linear Regression Association of Per Capita Agriculture Expenditures with Enset Yield

Log Linear Regression
Dependent variable: Enset Yield

Independent variables:	OLS
Log yearly expenditure per capita in Agriculture	2.397***
	(0. 5766)
Percentage of rural population	−1.091
	(1.7449)
Rainfall controls	
Average rainfall	0.000
	(0.0011)
Deviation from average rainfall	0.010
	(0.0168)
Deviation from average rainfall (lagged)	0.068***
	(0.0157)
Regional dummies	
Tigray	Omitted
Afar	Omitted
Amhara	Omitted
Oromia	8.654***
	(3.0691)
Somali	Omitted
Beneshangul Gemuz	Omitted
SNNP	1.357
	(1.4055)
Gambella	Omitted
Regional dummies × average rainfall	
Tigray × average rainfall	Omitted
Afar × average rainfall	Omitted
Amhara × average rainfall	Omitted
Oromia × average rainfall	−0.005***
	(0.0016)
Somali × average rainfall	Omitted
Beneshangul Gemuz × average rainfall	Omitted
SNNP × average rainfall	Omitted
Gambella × average rainfall	Omitted

table continues next page

Table D.24 Stage 1: Agriculture—Log Linear Regression Association of Per Capita Agriculture Expenditures with Enset Yield *(continued)*

Regional dummies × Poverty rate	
Tigray × Poverty rate	Omitted
Afar × Poverty rate	Omitted
Amhara × Poverty rate	Omitted
Oromia × Poverty rate	−0.034
	(0.0527)
Somali × Poverty rate	Omitted
Beneshangul Gemuz × Poverty rate	Omitted
SNNP × Poverty rate	0.020***
	(4.3094)
Gambella × Poverty rate	−1.044*
	(0.7084)
Constant	−13.452***
	(4.3094)

Note: Cross-time pooled regressions with robust standard errors; standard errors in parentheses; *, **, *** = coefficients significant at the 10 percent, 5 percent and 1 percent levels. OLS = ordinary least squares; SNNP = Southern Nations, Nationalities, and Peoples (Region). Dire Dawa and Hara omitted due to small scale of agriculture in these regions

Table D.25 Stage 1: Agriculture—Log Linear Regression Association of Per Capita Agriculture Expenditures with Fruit Yield

Log Linear Regression
Dependent variable: Fruit Yield

Independent variables:	OLS
Log yearly expenditure per capita in Agriculture	1.790***
	(0.2669)
Percentage of rural population	−0.794
	(0.9149)
Rainfall controls	
Average rainfall	0.000
	(0.0006)
Deviation from average rainfall	0.002
	(0.0048)
Deviation from average rainfall (lagged)	0.028***
	(0.0050)
Regional dummies	
Tigray	−2.459
	(3.3924)
Afar	4.850*
	(2.8878)
Amhara	−0.309
	(0.9558)
Oromia	2.933**
	(1.2536)
Somali	−5.032
	(6.4944)
Beneshangul Gemuz	−108.598**
	(55.213)
SNNP	Omitted
Gambella	Omitted
Regional dummies × average rainfall	
Tigray × average rainfall	0.001
	(0.0019)
Afar × average rainfall	−0.009
	(0.0059)
Amhara × average rainfall	0.001
	(0.0013)
Oromia × average rainfall	−0.002**
	(0.0008)
Somali × average rainfall	0.005
	(0.0090)

table continues next page

Table D.25 Stage 1: Agriculture—Log Linear Regression Association of Per Capita Agriculture Expenditures with Fruit Yield (continued)

Beneshangul Gemuz × average rainfall	0.087*
	(0.0448)
SNNP × average rainfall	Omitted
Gambella × average rainfall	Omitted
Regional dummies × Poverty rate	
Tigray × Poverty rate	0.002
	(0.0665)
Afar × Poverty rate	Omitted
Amhara × Poverty rate	−0.023
	(0.0213)
Oromia × Poverty rate	−0.019
	(0.0267)
Somali × Poverty rate	0.113
	(0.0727)
Beneshangul Gemuz × Poverty rate	0.288*
	(0.1537)
SNNP × Poverty rate	0.014
	(0.0093)
Gambella × Poverty rate	Omitted
Constant	−4.019***
	(1.4968)

Note: Cross-time pooled regressions with robust standard errors; standard errors in parentheses; * , **, *** = coefficients significant at the 10 percent, 5 percent and 1 percent levels. OLS = ordinary least squares; SNNP = Southern Nations, Nationalities, and Peoples (Region). Dire Dawa and Hara omitted due to small scale of agriculture in these regions

Table D.26 Stage 1: Agriculture—Log Linear Regression Association of Per Capita Agriculture Expenditures with Coffee Yield

Log Linear Regression
Dependent variable: Coffee Yield

Independent variables:	OLS
Log yearly expenditure per capita in Agriculture	1.267***
	(0. 2342)
Percentage of rural population	−0.777
	(0.7845)
Rainfall controls	
Average rainfall	0.000
	(0.0005)
Deviation from average rainfall	−0.001
	(0.0048)
Deviation from average rainfall (lagged)	0.029***
	(0.0049)
Regional dummies	
Tigray	Omitted
Afar	Omitted
Amhara	−0.632
	(0.8110)
Oromia	2.014*
	(1.0696)
Somali	1.43**
	(0.6380)
Beneshangul Gemuz	−18.760
	(46.6977)
SNNP	Omitted
Gambella	Omitted
Regional dummies × average rainfall	
Tigray × average rainfall	Omitted
Afar × average rainfall	Omitted
Amhara × average rainfall	0.000
	(0.0011)
Oromia × average rainfall	−0.001***
	(0.0007)
Somali × average rainfall	Omitted
Beneshangul Gemuz × average rainfall	0.014
	(0.0379)
SNNP × average rainfall	Omitted
Gambella × average rainfall	Omitted

table continues next page

Table D.26 Stage 1: Agriculture—Log Linear Regression Association of Per Capita Agriculture Expenditures with Coffee Yield (continued)

Regional dummies × Poverty rate	
Tigray × Poverty rate	Omitted
Afar × Poverty rate	Omitted
Amhara × Poverty rate	−0.012
	(0.0180)
Oromia × Poverty rate	0.004
	(0.0228)
Somali × Poverty rate	Omitted
Beneshangul Gemuz × Poverty rate	0.068
	(0.1300)
SNNP × Poverty rate	0.007
	(0.0082)
Gambella × Poverty rate	Omitted
Constant	−4.095***
	(1.3591)

Note: Cross-time pooled regressions with robust standard errors; standard errors in parentheses; *, **, *** = coefficients significant at the 10 percent, 5 percent and 1 percent levels. OLS = ordinary least squares; SNNP = Southern Nations, Nationalities, and Peoples (Region). Dire Dawa and Hara omitted due to small scale of agriculture in these regions

Table D.27 Stage 3: Agriculture—Predicted Probabilities for Farmers' Use of Any Improved Technique, 2011

Dependent variable: Any Improved Technique, 2011

Independent variables:	Probit	Predicted Probability
Yearly expenditure per capita in Agriculture	0.0033	
	(0.00029)	
Poverty rate	0.0075**	
	(0.00295)	
Rainfall controls		
Average rainfall	−0.00078***	
	(0.00007)	
Deviation from average rainfall 2011	−0.00306***	
	(0.00046)	
Deviation from average rainfall 2010	0.0090***	
	(0.00043)	
Regional dummies		
Tigray	omitted	
Afar	−5.1478***	
	(0.58951)	
Amhara	−2.8538***	
	(0.13734)	
Oromia	−0.02614	
	(0.14042)	
Somali	−1.1050	
	(2.79749)	
Beneshangul Gemuz	−28.8422***	
	(5.38058)	
SNNP	−0.9599	
	(0.14272)	
Gambella	40.0622	
Regional dummies × average rainfall		
Tigray × average rainfall	omitted	
Afar × average rainfall	omitted	
Amhara × average rainfall	0.0031***	
	(0.00007)	
Oromia × average rainfall	−0.00001	
	(0.00007)	
Somali × average rainfall	−0.0025	
	(0.00408)	
Beneshangul Gemuz × average rainfall	0.0234***	
	(0.00434)	

table continues next page

Improving Basic Services for the Bottom Forty Percent • http://dx.doi.org/10.1596/978-1-4648-0331-4

Table D.27 Stage 3: Agriculture—Predicted Probabilities for Farmers' Use of Any Improved Technique, 2011 (continued)

SNNP × average rainfall	0.0005***	
	(0.00008)	
Gambella × average rainfall	0.0022***	
	0.00066	
Regional dummies × Poverty rate		
Tigray × Poverty rate	omitted	
Afar × Poverty rate	0.1298***	
	(0.01668)	
Amhara × Poverty rate	−0.0027	
	(0.00304)	
Oromia × Poverty rate	−0.0207***	
	(0.00307)	
Somali × Poverty rate	−0.0016	
	(0.02692)	
Beneshangul Gemuz × Poverty rate	0.0446***	
	(0.01563)	
SNNP × Poverty rate	−0.0010	
	(0.00298)	
Gambella × Poverty rate	−1.4040	
Quintile		
Smallest/Poorest	omitted	0.0003***
		(0.00002)
Second/Poorer	0.0445***	0.0003***
	(0.01386)	(0.00003)
Middle/Middle	0.3727***	0.0005***
	(0.01282)	(0.00004)
Fourth/Richer	0.5961***	0.0006***
	(0.01265)	(0.00005)
Largest/Richest	0.8211***	0.0008***
	(0.01280)	(0.00007)
Constant	−1.7225***	
	(0.15902)	

Note: Cross-time pooled regressions with robust standard errors; standard errors in parentheses; * , **, *** = coefficients significant at the 10 percent, 5 percent and 1 percent levels.

Table D.28 Gender Issues: Linear Regression Association of Per Capita Education Expenditures with Net Enrollment Rate for Males

Linear Regression

Dependent variable: Net Enrollment Rate—Male

Independent variables:	OLS
Yearly expenditure per capita in Education	0.0438***
	(0.0070)
Percentage of rural population	−7.011
	(5.71317)
Ethnicity controls	
Nuwer	6.7239
	(6.35115)
Anyiwak	−17.9619
	(13.65227)
Gumuz	2.1839
	(7.19484)
Konso	−34.8711*
	(19.43414)
Other Small	0.7764
	(3.70825)
Constant	84.8515***
	(5.20259)

Note: Cross-time pooled regressions with robust standard errors; standard errors in parentheses; * , **, *** = coefficients significant at the 10 percent, 5 percent and 1 percent levels. OLS = ordinary least squares.

Table D.29   Gender Issues: Quadratic Regression Association of Per Capita Education Expenditures with Net Enrollment Rate for Males

Quadratic Regression
Dependent variable: Net Enrollment Rate—Male

Independent variables:	OLS
Yearly expenditure per capita in Education	0.095***
	(0.0180)
Yearly expenditure per capita in Education Squared	−0.0001***
	(0.00005)
Percentage of rural population	−6.474
	(5.6910)
Ethnicity controls	
Nuwer	5.652
	(6.4082)
Anyiwak	−11.147
	(12.9711)
Gumuz	0.707
	(7.0657)
Konso	−34.690*
	(19.6667)
Other Small	0.632
	(3.6941)
Constant	81.002***
	(5.2059)

Note: Cross-time pooled regressions with robust standard errors; standard errors in parentheses; *, **, *** = coefficients significant at the 10 percent, 5 percent and 1 percent levels. OLS = ordinary least squares.

Table D.30   Gender Issues: Log Linear Regression Association of Per Capita Education Expenditures with Net Enrollment Rate for Males

Log Linear Regression
Dependent variable: Log Net Enrollment Rate—Male

Independent variables:	OLS
Log of yearly expenditure per capita in Education	0.115***
	(0.0116)
Constant	3.752***
	(0.0627)

Note: Cross-time pooled regressions with robust standard errors; standard errors in parentheses; *, **, *** = coefficients significant at the 10 percent, 5 percent and 1 percent levels. OLS = ordinary least squares.

Table D.31 Gender Issues: Linear Regression Association of Per Capita Education Expenditures with Net Enrollment Rate for Females

Dependent variable: Net Enrollment Rate—Female

Independent variables:	OLS
Yearly expenditure per capita in Education	0.0476***
	(0.00756)
Percentage of rural population	−12.2364**
	(5.53352)
Ethnicity controls	
Nuwer	−10.2088***
	(3.26873)
Anyiwak	−21.4472***
	(12.98825)
Gumuz	−22.8067***
	(8.07086)
Konso	−37.6488***
	(13.07193)
Other Small	−8.2162**
	(3.91541)
Constant	87.8880***
	(5.09835)

Note: Cross-time pooled regressions with robust standard errors; standard errors in parentheses; * , **, *** = coefficients significant at the 10 percent, 5 percent and 1 percent levels. OLS = ordinary least squares.

Table D.32 Gender Issues: Quadratic Regression Association of Per Capita Education Expenditures with Net Enrollment Rate for Females

Quadratic Regression

Dependent variable: Net Enrollment Rate—Female

Independent variables:	OLS
Yearly expenditure per capita in Education	0.095***
	(0.0180)
Yearly expenditure per capita in Education Squared	−0.0001***
	(0.00005)
Percentage of rural population	−11.682**
	(5.5100)
Ethnicity controls	
Nuwer	−11.325***
	(3.3056)
Anyiwak	−14.655
	(12.271)
Gumuz	−24.307***
	(7.9683)
Konso	−37.462***
	(13.3247)

table continues next page

Table D.32 Gender Issues: Quadratic Regression Association of Per Capita Education Expenditures with Net Enrollment Rate for Females *(continued)*

Other Small	−8.355**
	(3.8904)
Constant	81.002***
	(5.2059)

Note: Cross-time pooled regressions with robust standard errors; standard errors in parentheses; * , **, *** = coefficients significant at the 10 percent, 5 percent and 1 percent levels. OLS = ordinary least squares.

Table D.33 Gender Issues: Log Linear Regression Association of Per Capita Education Expenditures with Net Enrollment Rate for Females

Log Linear Regression
Dependent variable: Log Net Enrollment Rate—Female

Independent variables:	OLS
Log of yearly expenditure per capita in Education	0.158***
	(0.0137)
Constant	3.505***
	(0.0746)

Note: Cross-time pooled regressions with robust standard errors; standard errors in parentheses; * , **, *** = coefficients significant at the 10 percent, 5 percent and 1 percent levels. OLS = ordinary least squares.

Table D.34 Gender Issues: Linear Regression Association of Per Capita Education Expenditures with Net Intake Rate for Males

Dependent variable: Net Intake Rate—Male

Independent variables:	OLS
Yearly expenditure per capita in Education	0.1670***
	(0.01702)
Percentage of rural population	31.6473***
	(5.71317)
Ethnicity controls	
Nuwer	−74.3077***
	(5.43405)
Anyiwak	−95.4275***
	(20.37484)
Gumuz	−54.9533***
	(11.42498)
Konso	−27.4514
	(22.54912)
Other Small	−3.7305
	(4.52154)
Constant	43.4391***
	(6.55315)

Note: Cross-time pooled regressions with robust standard errors; standard errors in parentheses; * , **, *** = coefficients significant at the 10 percent, 5 percent and 1 percent levels. OLS = ordinary least squares.

Table D.35 Gender Issues: Quadratic Regression Association of Per Capita Education Expenditures with Net Intake Rate for Males

Quadratic Regression

Dependent variable: Net Intake Rate—Male

Independent variables:	OLS
Yearly expenditure per capita in Education	0.418***
	(0.0275
Yearly expenditure per capita in Education Squared	−0.0006***
	(0.00007)
Percentage of rural population	34.070***
	(6.8756)
Ethnicity controls	
Nuwer	−81.015***
	(4.4688)
Anyiwak	−64.507***
	(11.3181)
Gumuz	−61.676***
	(11.3097)
Konso	−29.614
	(22.6827)
Other Small	−4.308
	(4.5489)
Constant	24.648***
	(6.1562)

Note: Cross-time pooled regressions with robust standard errors; standard errors in parentheses; * , ** , *** = coefficients significant at the 10 percent, 5 percent and 1 percent levels. OLS = ordinary least squares.

Table D.36 Gender Issues: Log Linear Regression Association of Per Capita Education Expenditures with Net Intake Rate for Males

Log Linear Regression

Dependent variable: Log Net Intake Rate—Male

Independent variables:	OLS
Log of yearly expenditure per capita in Education	0.390***
	(0.0240)
Constant	2.420***
	(0.1202)

Note: Cross-time pooled regressions with robust standard errors; standard errors in parentheses; * , ** , *** = coefficients significant at the 10 percent, 5 percent and 1 percent levels. OLS = ordinary least squares.

Table D.37   Gender Issues: Linear Regression Association of Per Capita Education Expenditures with Net Intake Rate for Females

Dependent variable: Net Intake Rate—Female

Independent variables:	OLS
Yearly expenditure per capita in Education	0.16698***
	(0.01642)
Percentage of rural population	0.0476***
	(6.51252)
Ethnicity controls	
Nuwer	−71.7297***
	(5.09329)
Anyiwak	−93.7788***
	(20.3585)
Gumuz	−61.4025***
	(9.81233)
Konso	−18.8002
	(18.30648)
Other Small	−10.58377**
	(4.31694)
Constant	44.9443***
	(6.10655)

Note: Cross-time pooled regressions with robust standard errors; standard errors in parentheses; *, **, *** = coefficients significant at the 10 percent, 5 percent and 1 percent levels. OLS = ordinary least squares.

Table D.38   Gender Issues: Quadratic Regression Association of Per Capita Education Expenditures with Net Intake Rate for Females

Quadratic Regression
Dependent variable: Net Intake Rate—Female

Independent variables:	OLS
Yearly expenditure per capita in Education	0.404***
	(0.0273)
Yearly expenditure per capita in Education Squared	−0.0006***
	(.00007)
Percentage of rural population	28.551***
	(6.2956)
Ethnicity controls	
Nuwer	−78.070***
	(4.2173)
Anyiwak	−64.674***
	(11.6827)
Gumuz	−67.738***
	(9.8523)
Konso	−20.859
	(18.5272)

table continues next page

Table D.38   Gender Issues: Quadratic Regression Association of Per Capita Education Expenditures with Net Intake Rate for Females (continued)

Other Small	−11.122**
	(4.3080)
Constant	27.221***
	(5.7160)

Note: Cross-time pooled regressions with robust standard errors; standard errors in parentheses; * , **, *** = coefficients significant at the 10 percent, 5 percent and 1 percent levels. OLS = ordinary least squares.

Table D.39   Gender Issues: Log Linear Regression Association of Per Capita Education Expenditures with Net Intake Rate for Females

Log Linear Regression
Dependent variable: Log Net Intake Rate—Female

Independent variables:	OLS
Log of yearly expenditure per capita in Education	0.430***
	(.0269)
Constant	2.183***
	(0.1354)

Note: Cross-time pooled regressions with robust standard errors; standard errors in parentheses; * , **, *** = coefficients significant at the 10 percent, 5 percent and 1 percent levels. OLS = ordinary least squares.

Table D.40   Gender Issues: Predicted Probabilities for Farmers' Use of Any Improved Technique by Gender, 2011

Dependent variable: Any Improved Technique by gender, 2011

Independent variables:	Probit	Predicted Probability
Yearly expenditure per capita in Agriculture	0.0019	
	(0.00032)	
Poverty rate	0.0089***	
	(0.00285)	
Rainfall controls		
Average rainfall	−0.00060***	
	(0.00007)	
Deviation from average rainfall 2011	−0.00379***	
	(0.00046)	
Deviation from average rainfall 2010	0.0090***	
	(0.00043)	
Regional dummies		
Tigray	omitted	
Afar	−5.9148***	
	(0.57195)	
Amhara	−2.8286***	
	(0.13357)	
Oromia	0.32604	
	(0.13683)	

table continues next page

Table D.40   Gender Issues: Predicted Probabilities for Farmers' Use of Any Improved Technique by Gender, 2011 *(continued)*

Somali	−1.5086
	(2.71172)
Beneshangul Gemuz	−33.9580***
	(5.17708)
SNNP	−0.0528
	(0.14926)
Gambella	43.2032
Regional dummies × average rainfall	
Tigray × average rainfall	omitted
Afar × average rainfall	omitted
Amhara × average rainfall	0.0031***
	(0.00007)
Oromia × average rainfall	−0.00036
	(0.00007)
Somali × average rainfall	−0.0058
	(0.00395)
Beneshangul Gemuz × average rainfall	0.0277***
	(0.00418)
SNNP × average rainfall	0.0028***
	(0.00008)
Gambella × average rainfall	0.0013***
	0.00081
Regional dummies × Poverty rate	
Tigray × Poverty rate	omitted
Afar × Poverty rate	0.1515***
	(0.01644)
Amhara × Poverty rate	−0.0071
	(0.00295)
Oromia × Poverty rate	−0.0207***
	(0.00297)
Somali × Poverty rate	−0.0369
	(0.02617)
Beneshangul Gemuz × Poverty rate	0.0528***
	(0.01504)
SNNP × Poverty rate	−0.0040
	(0.00298)
Gambella × Poverty rate	−1.4770

table continues next page

Table D.40 Gender Issues: Predicted Probabilities for Farmers' Use of Any Improved Technique by Gender, 2011 *(continued)*

Sex		
Male	0.0002***	0.00003***
		(0.00000)
Female	−0.0001***	−0.00002***
	(0.00001)	(0.00000)
Constant	−1.2469***	
	(0.15362)	

Note: Probit regressions with robust standard errors in parentheses; Predicted probabilities with unconditional standard errors in parentheses. *, **, *** = coefficients significant at the 10 percent, 5 percent and 1 percent levels. SNNP = Southern Nations, Nationalities, and Peoples (Region). Dire Dawa and Hara omitted due to small scale of agriculture in these regions.

Bibliography

Adegehe, Asnake. 2009. "Federalism and Ethnic Conflict in Ethiopia: A Comparative Study of the Somali and Benishangul-Gumuz Regions." Doctoral thesis, Department of Political Science, Faculty of Social and Behavioural Sciences, Leiden University.

Assefa, Fisshea. 2010. *Federalism and the Accommodation of Diversity in Ethiopia*. 3rd ed. Addis Ababa: Eclipse Press.

Barankay, I., and B. Lockwood. 2007. "Decentralization and the Productive Efficiency of Government: Evidence from Swiss Cantons." *Journal of Public Economics* 91 (5–6): 1197–218.

Batina, R. G., and T. Ihori. 2005. *Public Goods: Theories and Evidence*. New York: Springer.

Besley, T., and S. Coate. 2003. "Centralized versus Decentralized Provision of Local Public Goods: A Political Economy Approach." *Journal of Public Economics* 87 (12): 2611–37.

Bevan, Phillipa, Catherine Dom, and Alula Pankhurst. 2010. "Long-term Perspectives of Development Impacts in Rural Ethiopia: Wide Stage One Final Report." Mokoro Limited, Oxford.

Boone, P., and J. P. Faguet. 1998. "Multilateral Aid, Politics, and Poverty: Past Failures and Future Challenges." Chapter 2 in *The Global Crisis in Foreign Aid*, edited by R. Grant and J. Nijman, 11–26. Syracuse: Syracuse University Press.

Cassette, A., and S. Paty. 2010. "Fiscal Decentralization and the Size of Government: A European Country Empirical Analysis." *Public Choice* 143 (1–2): 173–89.

Ceballos, M., and D. Hoyos. 2004. "Tendencias del comportamiento electoraly descentralización en los municipios de Colombia, 1988–2000." Crisis States Programme Working Paper No. 57, London School of Economics.

Clapham, Christopher. 1994. "Ethnicity and the National Question in Ethiopia." In *Conflict and Peace in the Horn of Africa: Federalism and Its Alternatives*, edited by Peter Woodward and Murray Forsyth, 27–40. Aldershot: Dartmouth Publishing.

Clark, D. 2009. "The Performance and Competitive Effects of School Autonomy." *Journal of Political Economy* 117 (4): 745–82.

CSA (Central Statistical Agency of Ethiopia). "Voice of the Central Statistical Agency." Various issues. Addis Ababa.

Devarajan, S., S. Khemani, and S. Shah. 2009. "The Politics of Partial Decentralization." In *Does Decentralization Enhance Service Delivery and Poverty Reduction?* edited by E. Ahmad and G. Brosio. Cheltenham: Edward Elgar.

Dowding, K., and P. John. 1994. "Tiebout: A Survey of the Empirical Literature." *Urban Studies* 31 (4/5): 767–97.

Dom, Catherine, and Stephen Lister, with Manos Antoninis. 2010. "An Analysis of Decentralization in Ethiopia." Mokoro Limited, Oxford.

Eldon, Jack, Abebe, Cunningham, and Bibby. 2011. "Options for Support to Service Delivery in Ethiopia's Developing Regional States."

Escaleras, M., and C. A. Register. 2012. "Fiscal Decentralization and Natural Hazard Risks." *Public Choice* 151 (1): 165–83.

Faguet, J. P. 2000. "Decentralization and Local Government Performance: Improving Public Service Provision in Bolivia." *Revista de Economía del Rosario* 3 (1): 127–76.

———. 2004. "Why So Much Centralization? A Model of Primitive Centripetal Accumulation." LSE-STICERD Development Economics Discussion Paper No. 43, London School of Economics.

———. 2012. *Decentralization and Popular Democracy: Governance from Below in Bolivia.* Ann Arbor: University of Michigan.

———. 2014. "Decentralization and Governance." *World Development* 53: 2–13.

Faguet, J. P., and Z. Ali. 2009. "Making Reform Work: Institutions, Dispositions, and the Improving Health of Bangladesh." *World Development* 37 (1): 208–18.

Faguet, J. P., and F. Sánchez. 2013. "Decentralization and Access to Social Services in Colombia." *Public Choice.* doi: 10.1007/s11127-013-0077-7.

Faguet, J. P., and F. B. Wietzke. 2006. "Social Funds and Decentralization: Optimal Institutional Design." *Public Administration and Development* 26 (4): 303–15.

Galiani, S., P. Gertler, and D. Schargrodsky. 2008. "School Decentralization: Helping the Good Get Better, but Leaving the Poor Behind." *Journal of Public Economics* 92 (10–11): 2106–20.

Garcia, Marito, and Andrew Sunil Rajkumar. 2008. "Achieving Better Service Delivery through Decentralization in Ethiopia." African Human Development Series Working Paper No. 131, World Bank, Washington, DC.

Gonçalves, S. 2013. "The Effects of Participatory Budgeting on Municipal Expenditures and Infant Mortality in Brazil." *World Development.* http://dx.doi.org/10.1016/j.worlddev.2013.01.009.

Granados, C., and F. Sánchez. 2014. "Water Reforms, Decentralization, and Child Mortality in Colombia, 1990–2005." *World Development* 53 (C): 68–79.

IPE Global. 2010. "Evaluation and Design of the Social Accountability Component of the Protection of Basic Services Project." New Delhi.

Kamurase, Alex, and Aly Salman Alibhai. 2014. "Social Accountability for Ethiopia PBS." Presentation for session on Tricks and Tools of Task Team Leaders, Sustainable Development Network Forum, World Bank, Washington, DC, February.

Krishan, Pramila, and Manasa Patnam. 2013. "Neighbours and Extension Agents in Ethiopia: Who Matters More?" *American Journal of Agricultural Economics* 96 (1): 308–27.

Manor, J. 1999. *The Political Economy of Democratic Decentralization.* Washington, DC: World Bank.

Meles, Zenawi. 1997. "Premier's Speech at Butare National University in Rwanda." *Ethiopian Herald*, December 13.

Mulugeta, Allehone. 2002. "Issues of Security and Conflict, in the Ethiopian Frontiers: Notes on State Policies and Strategies." Report of Ethiopia National Workshop, Conflict in the Horn: Prevention and Resolution, Organization for Social Science Research in Eastern and Southern Africa (OSSREA), Addis Ababa.

Oates, W. 1972. *Fiscal Federalism*. New York: Harcourt Brace.

ODI (Overseas Development Institute). 2010. "Millennium Development Goals Report Card: Measuring Progress Across Countries." London.

Ostrom, E., L. Schroeder, and S. Wynne. 1993. *Institutional Incentives and Sustainable Development: Infrastructure Policies in Perspective*. Boulder: Westview.

Ostrom, E., and G. P. Whitaker. 1973. "Does Local Community Control of Police Make a Difference? Some Preliminary Findings." *American Journal of Political Science* 17 (1): 48–76.

Piriou-Sall, S. 1998. "Decentralisation and Rural Development: A Review of Evidence." Washington, DC. Processed.

Prohl, S., and F. Schneider. 2009. "Does Decentralization Reduce Government Size? A Quantitative Study of the Decentralization Hypothesis." *Public Finance Review* 37 (6): 639–64.

Prud'homme, R. 1995. "On the Dangers of Decentralisation." *World Bank Research Observer* 10 (2): 210–26.

Putnam, R. D. 1993. *Making Democracy Work: Civic Traditions in Modern Italy*. Princeton: Princeton University.

Ragasa, Catherine, Guush Berhane, Fanayae Tadesse, and Alemayehu Seyoum Taffesse. 2012. "Gender Differences in Access to Extension Services and Agriculture Productivity." ESSP Working Paper No. 49, Ethiopia Strategy Support Program (ESSP), Ethiopia Development Research Institute (EDRI), and International Food Policy Research Institute (IFPRI), Washington, DC.

Randolph, Robert C., and Buli Edjeta. 2011. "Study on Strengthening Grievance Redress Mechanisms for the Protection of the Basic Services (PBS) Program in Ethiopia." Addis Ababa.

Rondinelli, D. A., G. S. Cheema, and J. Nellis. 1983. "Decentralisation in Developing Countries: A Review of Recent Experience." Staff Working Paper No. 581, World Bank, Washington, DC.

Samoff, J. 1990. "Decentralisation: The Politics of Interventionism." *Development and Change* 21 (3): 513–30.

Selam Development Consultants. 2013. "Financial Transparency and Accountability Implementation Assessment Report." Addis Ababa.

Smoke, P. 2001. "Fiscal Decentralisation in Developing Countries: A Review of Current Concepts and Practice." Democracy, Governance, and Human Rights Programme Paper No. 2, United Nations Research Institute for Social Development, Geneva.

Solomon, Negussie. 2008. "Fiscal Federalism in the Ethiopian Ethnic-based Federal System." Forum of Federations, Addis Ababa.

Tiebout, C. M. 1956. "A Pure Theory of Local Expenditures." *Journal of Political Economy* 64 (5): 416–24.

Treisman, D. 2007. *The Architecture of Government: Rethinking Political Decentralization*. New York: Cambridge University.

Vaillancourt, Francois. 2013. "Sharing Central Revenues with Regions: An Examination of Principles and Practices in the Context of the PBS (Ethiopia) Program." World Bank, Addis Ababa.

Vaughan, Sarah. 2012. "Understanding Ethiopia's Transformation: Vision and Strategies for Development." World Bank, Addis Ababa.

Wang, Huihui, G. N. V. Ramana, Jie Huang, and Bekele Chaka. Forthcoming. "Ethiopia Universal Health Care Case Study." World Bank, Washington, DC.

Weldemariam, Alemayehu F. 2011. "Greater Ethiopia: Evolution of a Pluralist Politico-Legal System in a Pluralist Polity." http://dx.doi.org/10.2139/ssrn.1909803.

Woldehanna, Tassew, Eyasu Tsehaye, and Ruth Hill. Forthcoming. "The Distributional Impact of Fiscal Policy in Ethiopia." Contribution to a Global Study of Fiscal Incidence led by Nora Lustig, World Bank, Washington, DC.

World Bank. 2003. *World Development Report 2004: Making Services Work for Poor People.* Washington, DC: World Bank.

———. 2010. "Financial Transparency and Accountability Initiative in Ethiopia: Progress and Way Forward." Addis Ababa.

———. 2011a. "An Assessment of Public Finance Management Systems in Woreda Governments." Addis Ababa.

———. 2011b. *Citizens and Service: Assessing Use of Social Accountability Approaches in the Human Development Sectors.* Directions in Development. Washington, DC: World Bank.

———. 2012a. "Project Appraisal Document for Ethiopia Promoting Basic Services Project Phase III." Report No. 69689-ET, World Bank, Washington, DC.

———. 2012b. "Serving the Ethiopian People: The Origins and Evolution of the PBS Programme." Working Paper No. 74851, World Bank, Washington, DC.

———. 2013. "Understanding Incentives and Strengthening Services: The Political Economy of Decentralized Delivery in Ethiopia." World Bank, Washington, DC.

———. 2014. "Improving Basic Services for the Bottom Forty Percent: Results of the Poverty and Social Impact Assessment of Decentralized Basic Service Delivery in Ethiopia." Report No: 84215-ET, World Bank, Washington, DC.

Yang, Jing. 2012. "Interpreting Coefficients in Regression with Log-Transformed Variables." *StatNews* No. 83 (June). Cornell Statistical Consulting Unit, Ithaca.

Zewde, Bahru. 1991. *A History of Modern Ethiopia 1855–1974.* Addis Ababa: Addis Ababa University Press.

Environmental Benefits Statement

The World Bank is committed to reducing its environmental footprint. In support of this commitment, the Publishing and Knowledge Division leverages electronic publishing options and print-on-demand technology, which is located in regional hubs worldwide. Together, these initiatives enable print runs to be lowered and shipping distances decreased, resulting in reduced paper consumption, chemical use, greenhouse gas emissions, and waste.

The Publishing and Knowledge Division follows the recommended standards for paper use set by the Green Press Initiative. Whenever possible, books are printed on 50 percent to 100 percent postconsumer recycled paper, and at least 50 percent of the fiber in our book paper is either unbleached or bleached using Totally Chlorine Free (TCF), Processed Chlorine Free (PCF), or Enhanced Elemental Chlorine Free (EECF) processes.

More information about the Bank's environmental philosophy can be found at http://crinfo.worldbank.org/wbcrinfo/node/4.

green press INITIATIVE